ROUTE 66
TRAVEL GUIDE
2025

DONALD E TURNER

TABLE OF CONTENTS

INTRODUCTION

Route 66, often called the Mother Road, is more than just a highway; it's a journey through America's heart. Stretching over 2,400 miles from Chicago to Santa Monica, this historic route is filled with stories, nostalgia, and a unique charm that captures the spirit of adventure. As I set out on this journey, I was eager to experience the magic that so many had talked about.

I'd always been a bit of a daredevil. When a friend suggested a spontaneous road trip along Route 66 as a dare, I jumped at the chance. I'd actually been planning a trip to visit Las Vegas (a story for my other guide), so I decided to start my adventure here, embracing the full Route 66 experience from the get-go. I'd heard about the Mother Road, of course, but I'd never really given it much thought. My online research hinted at a nostalgic, historic highway, but nothing prepared me for the magic I was about to encounter.

Driving down this iconic stretch of asphalt, I felt a surge of excitement. The landscape transformed before my eyes, showcasing vibrant red rocks in Arizona and endless blue skies over Oklahoma. Small towns dotted the way, each feeling like a step back in time with their vintage diners, classic car shops, and welcoming locals.

One of my favorite moments was a detour to Cadillac Ranch, a quirky roadside attraction where several Cadillacs stand half-buried in the ground. I couldn't resist adding my own graffiti to one of the cars, leaving a piece of myself on this iconic landmark.

Another unforgettable experience was staying at the Wigwam Motel in Holbrook, Arizona. This unique motel features rooms shaped like teepees, offering a fun and nostalgic lodging experience that added to the adventure.

But what made Route 66 truly special wasn't just the famous attractions. It was the sense of adventure, the thrill of the open road, and the unexpected surprises that made this journey unforgettable. I found myself stopping at roadside attractions, exploring ghost towns, and simply soaking in the beauty of the American landscape.

As I drove away from Route 66, I realized this trip was more than just a road trip; it was a journey of self-discovery and a celebration of the American spirit. I felt compelled to share my love for this hidden gem with others. This travel guide aims to inspire you to explore the magic of Route 66, revealing the wonders and experiences that await along this iconic road.

So buckle up and get ready to discover the charm and adventure that Route 66 has to offer. Each chapter will lead you through the hidden treasures, unforgettable experiences, and vibrant history of this legendary highway. Let's hit the road together and embrace the journey ahead!

The History of Route 66

Route 66 has a rich history that is deeply woven into the fabric of American culture. Often called the Mother Road, this highway was established in 1926, connecting Chicago to Santa Monica. It was one of the first major highways in the United States and served as a crucial route for those traveling westward. The road quickly became a symbol of freedom and adventure, attracting families and travelers looking for new opportunities and experiences.

During the Great Depression in the 1930s, Route 66 played an important role in helping people escape the hardships of their lives. Many families left their homes in search of a better future, driving along this highway in search of work and a fresh start. The road was filled with stories of struggle and resilience, as people set out on journeys that changed their lives forever. Towns along Route 66 became lifelines, offering food, shelter, and hope to those passing through.

The post-World War II era brought even more travelers to Route 66. With the rise of the automobile culture in America, more families hit the road for vacations and road trips. The highway was lined with roadside attractions, diners, motels, and gas stations that welcomed visitors with open arms. Classic diners served hearty meals, and quirky roadside stops offered fun experiences, such as giant sculptures and unique museums. Each stop had its own charm, making the journey just as exciting as the destination.

However, as time went on, the construction of the Interstate Highway System in the 1950s changed the way people traveled. Many parts of Route 66 were bypassed or neglected as drivers began to favor faster routes. This shift led to a decline in the towns along the highway, and some even faded away, losing their connection to the bustling road that once brought them life.

Despite this decline, Route 66 never lost its allure. In the 1980s, a renewed interest in this historic highway began to grow. People started to appreciate the nostalgia and the stories behind the road. Efforts were made to preserve the towns and attractions along Route 66, ensuring that the history and culture would not be forgotten. Restoration projects brought new life to old motels and diners, inviting travelers to experience the unique charm of the road once again.

Today, Route 66 stands as a testament to American history and adventure. It invites travelers to explore its winding path, discover hidden gems, and connect with the past. Each mile tells a story, from the scenic landscapes to the friendly faces you'll encounter along the way. Whether you're visiting classic diners, quirky roadside attractions, or simply soaking in the beauty of the journey, Route 66 offers a unique experience that celebrates the spirit of the open road.

Traveling along Route 66 is more than just a drive; it's a journey through time. Embrace the adventure, and let the stories of the past inspire your travels. There's a magic that awaits on this iconic highway, and it's a journey you won't want to miss.

Cultural Significance

Route 66 is not just a road; it is a symbol of American culture and history. This famous highway represents the dreams and adventures of countless people who traveled along its path. It has been a place where stories come to life, where traditions are celebrated, and where the spirit of exploration thrives.

One of the most significant aspects of Route 66 is how it connects people. From its early days, the road brought together families seeking a better life during difficult times. As people traveled westward, they shared their hopes and dreams, creating a sense of community along the way. The towns that popped up along the route became gathering places where travelers could meet, eat, and share their stories. The hospitality of locals and the welcoming atmosphere of diners and motels added to the charm of the journey.

Route 66 has also played a vital role in the growth of American music and art. Many musicians have been inspired by the road, creating songs that capture the essence of travel and adventure. Blues, rock, and country music often tell stories of life on the road, reflecting the experiences of those who journeyed along Route 66. The influence of these musical styles can be felt in the towns along the highway, where you can often find live performances that celebrate this rich cultural heritage.

Art is another important part of the Route 66 experience. From vibrant murals to roadside sculptures, creativity can be found at every turn. Many towns have embraced their history by commissioning artists to create works that pay homage to the road and its significance. These artworks tell the stories of the people and places along Route 66, capturing the unique character of each community. Taking the time to explore these artistic expressions adds depth to your journey and helps you connect with the culture of the area.

The cultural significance of Route 66 extends beyond its history and art. The highway has become a symbol of freedom and adventure, representing the open road and the endless possibilities that come with it. Many people find inspiration in the idea of hitting the road and discovering new places. This spirit of adventure encourages travelers to embrace the unknown, take risks, and explore the beauty of the American landscape.

As you travel along Route 66, you'll notice the celebrations and festivals that highlight the culture of the areas you pass through. Local events often showcase traditional food, music, and crafts that reflect the unique heritage of each community. Participating in these festivities gives you a deeper understanding of the culture and creates lasting memories.

Route 66 is more than just a route to your destination; it's an experience that allows you to connect with the heart of America. The stories, music, art, and traditions you encounter along the way will enrich your journey and inspire you to explore further. Embrace the cultural significance of this iconic highway, and let it guide you on an unforgettable adventure filled with discovery and connection.

Overview of the Route

Route 66 stretches over 2,400 miles, winding its way from Chicago, Illinois, to Santa Monica, California. This iconic highway takes you through a variety of landscapes, small towns, and big cities, each offering unique experiences and stories. Driving along this road feels like taking a step back in time, as it is filled with charming diners, quirky roadside attractions, and beautiful scenery.

Starting in Chicago, the journey begins in a bustling city known for its deep-dish pizza and impressive skyline. Here, you can explore famous sites like Millennium Park and the Art Institute of Chicago before hitting the open road. As you leave the city, the highway leads you through the flat lands of Illinois, where small towns dot the landscape. You can stop at cozy diners for a bite to eat and enjoy the friendly atmosphere.

As you continue west, you'll enter Missouri, where the route takes you through St. Louis. The iconic Gateway Arch stands tall here, representing the westward expansion of the United States. This city is a great place to grab a meal and take in some history before moving on. The drive through Missouri showcases rolling hills and lush landscapes, making it a scenic part of the journey.

Moving into Kansas, you'll experience a short stretch of Route 66, but it's packed with charm. This state is home to quirky roadside attractions, like the famous Carthage Route 66 Mural, which tells the story of the highway through colorful art. It's a perfect spot to stop, take pictures, and appreciate the creativity of the local community.

Oklahoma is next on the route, where you'll find a rich blend of history and culture. The route leads you through cities like Tulsa and Oklahoma City, where you can explore museums, art galleries, and unique local shops. The beautiful landscapes of Oklahoma include wide-open skies and rolling plains, inviting you to take in the beauty of the American heartland.

As you cross into Texas, the scenery shifts to the vast desert landscapes of the Panhandle. The towns here, like Amarillo, are known for their classic roadside attractions, including the famous Cadillac Ranch, where you can add your own graffiti to the half-buried cars. This area has a distinct Western feel, offering a taste of cowboy culture and traditions.

Continuing west, you'll enter New Mexico, where the landscape becomes even more dramatic. The vibrant colors of the desert and the rugged mountains create a stunning backdrop for your journey. Towns like Santa Fe are rich in art and history, making them great stops to explore local galleries and taste authentic Southwestern cuisine.

Arizona is a highlight of Route 66, filled with breathtaking sights. You can visit the Grand Canyon, one of the world's natural wonders, or stop in Flagstaff to enjoy the cool mountain air. The Route 66 towns in Arizona are filled with history, and you can discover the old trading posts and motels that once welcomed travelers on their way to California.

You'll reach California, where Route 66 leads you to the beautiful beaches of Santa Monica. The famous pier marks the end of the highway, where you can relax and enjoy the ocean. This final destination is a fitting conclusion to your journey, offering a chance to reflect on the adventures and memories made along the way.

Driving along Route 66 is more than just a road trip; it's a journey through the heart of America. Each mile brings new experiences, stories, and sights that celebrate the spirit of adventure. Whether you're stopping at classic diners, exploring historic towns, or enjoying the natural beauty of the landscapes, Route 66 promises an unforgettable adventure filled with charm and discovery.

Why visit Route 66?

Visiting Route 66 is like stepping into a living piece of history. This famous highway offers a unique journey filled with exciting experiences and unforgettable sights. There are many reasons to hit the road and explore this iconic route.

First, Route 66 takes you through beautiful landscapes. You will see everything from wide-open plains to stunning mountains and colorful deserts. Each state along the route has its own charm and scenery. Whether you're driving through the rolling hills of Missouri or the dramatic deserts of Arizona, the natural beauty will leave you in awe. Taking the time to enjoy the scenery can create a peaceful and refreshing experience.

Another reason to visit Route 66 is the chance to explore small towns that hold a lot of character. Each town along the way has its own unique stories, shops, and friendly locals. You can stop at vintage diners for a classic meal, browse local shops for handmade souvenirs, or chat with residents who have lived there for years. These interactions can make your trip feel personal and memorable.

Route 66 is also filled with quirky roadside attractions that add a sense of fun to your journey. From the famous Cadillac Ranch in Texas, where cars are half-buried and covered in graffiti, to the Route 66 Museum in New Mexico, each stop is an adventure in itself. These attractions tell the story of the road and create photo opportunities that you will cherish forever.

The rich history along Route 66 is another reason to visit. This road has witnessed countless stories of adventure, struggle, and triumph. It was once a main route for families moving west during the Great Depression, and its legacy lives on in the stories of those who traveled it. By exploring museums and historical sites, you can learn about the impact this highway has had on American culture and the people who traveled it.

Food is another highlight of a trip along Route 66. You will find classic diners, food trucks, and local eateries serving up delicious dishes that reflect the region's culture. Enjoy a slice of homemade pie, a hearty burger, or regional specialties that you won't find anywhere else. Each meal can be a delightful experience, connecting you to the local community through its flavors.

For many, Route 66 represents freedom and adventure. Driving along this highway allows you to feel the open road beneath your wheels and the wind in your hair. The sense of adventure encourages you to explore new places and create your own stories. Whether you're traveling solo, with friends, or with family, the journey becomes a shared experience filled with laughter and discovery.

Visiting Route 66 gives you a chance to disconnect from the hustle and bustle of everyday life. The leisurely pace of a road trip allows you to take in the sights, enjoy the journey, and appreciate the small moments along the way. It's a wonderful opportunity to slow down and embrace the beauty of the world around you.

Route 66 is not just a road; it is a journey through time, culture, and adventure. The beautiful landscapes, charming towns, quirky attractions, rich history, and delicious food all come together to create an unforgettable experience. Whether you're a history buff, a foodie, or simply looking for a great adventure, Route 66 has something for everyone. So pack your bags, hit the road, and get ready to make memories that will last a lifetime.

CHAPTER 1
PLANNING YOUR TRIP

Best Times to Travel

The best time to travel Route 66 depends on what kind of experience you're looking for, as each season offers its own charm and challenges. Whether you're after perfect weather, lower prices, or simply a quieter experience, Route 66 has something to offer year-round. Here's a detailed look at what you can expect throughout the seasons along this iconic road.

In the spring, Route 66 comes alive with fresh colors and milder weather, making it one of the best times to travel. The landscapes, especially in states like Arizona and New Mexico, are a blend of blooming wildflowers and lush greenery after the winter rains. The temperatures are comfortable, generally ranging from the 50s to 70s in most parts of the route, making it perfect for outdoor exploration.

For a comfortable spring visit, pack light layers, as mornings can still be cool, but the afternoons warm up nicely. A good windbreaker and some sturdy walking shoes will come in handy for spontaneous detours to hiking trails or city walks.

Spring is also festival season along Route 66. Towns like Tulsa, Oklahoma, often host local events celebrating the history of the road and the communities it runs through. This is a great time to catch art fairs, classic car shows, and even live music events that give you a sense of the culture that has grown around the highway.

During spring, the crowds are moderate, and costs remain relatively low. Many travelers wait for summer to hit the road, which means you can enjoy a more relaxed pace without the higher prices of peak travel season. Hotel availability is also more flexible, so booking last-minute accommodations is not a big issue.

Compared to summer, spring offers cooler temperatures and fewer crowds, making it an ideal time for those who prefer a more peaceful experience without the heat.

Summer is the most popular time to visit Route 66. The road is packed with travelers, and the iconic stops, from the Cadillac Ranch in Texas to the Santa Monica Pier in California, are buzzing with activity. The weather is generally hot, with temperatures often hitting the 90s or even higher in desert areas like Arizona and New Mexico. However, the bright sunshine and long daylight hours make it perfect for a classic American road trip.

Because of the heat, it's essential to pack lightweight, breathable clothing and plenty of sunscreen. A good hat and sunglasses are also important to keep you cool and protected from the intense summer sun. Don't forget to bring plenty of water, especially when traveling through the desert stretches where services can be far between.

Summer is when many towns along Route 66 hold their biggest events. You'll find outdoor concerts, county fairs, and even Route 66-specific celebrations like the "Route 66

Summerfest" in Albuquerque, New Mexico. The lively atmosphere is part of the appeal, but it's worth planning ahead since hotels and motels tend to fill up quickly. Making reservations in advance is a good idea to ensure you have a place to stay, especially in popular spots like Santa Fe or Flagstaff.

Prices rise during the summer months due to the high demand. Hotels and attractions tend to be busier, and you'll need to be prepared for crowds, especially at popular stops. However, the energetic vibe and the full experience of Route 66 at its busiest are a major draw for many travelers.

If you compare summer to spring or autumn, you'll notice the higher temperatures and larger crowds. However, if you love the lively, bustling atmosphere of a classic road trip, summer is when Route 66 feels the most vibrant.

Autumn brings a quieter, more relaxed atmosphere to Route 66, making it one of the best-kept secrets for travelers. The summer heat begins to fade, and cooler, more comfortable temperatures return. The foliage changes color, especially in states like Illinois and Missouri, where the leaves turn vibrant shades of red, orange, and gold, making the journey even more scenic.

Autumn weather can vary, so it's wise to pack in layers. A light jacket is a good idea for the cooler evenings, and comfortable shoes are a must for walking around the historic towns. Be prepared for occasional rain, especially in the Midwest, where showers are more frequent during this time of year.

Fall is also harvest season, which means many towns host food festivals celebrating the local produce. In Illinois, for example, you can enjoy fall festivals that feature apple picking, pumpkin patches, and local farmers' markets. These events give you a taste of the local flavor and make for fun stops along the way.

Crowds thin out in autumn, and prices begin to drop after the busy summer season. This is a great time to visit if you prefer a quieter, less crowded experience. Many accommodations offer off-season rates, so you can find deals on hotels and motels. Availability is less of a concern, and you'll often have more flexibility in your travel plans.

Compared to summer, autumn is cooler, less crowded, and offers a more laid-back experience. It's ideal for travelers who want to take their time and enjoy the road without the hustle and bustle of peak season.

Winter on Route 66 is the quietest time to travel. While the highway takes on a different kind of beauty in the winter months, with snow-dusted landscapes in some areas and crisp, clear air in others, it's not as popular due to the colder weather and the chance of road closures in snowy regions.

In northern parts of the route, especially in Illinois, Missouri, and northern New Mexico, snow can be common. Roads might be icy, and some attractions may close for the season. However, the southern stretches, particularly through Arizona and California, stay relatively mild, making winter a great time to explore the desert regions.

Winter travelers should pack warmly, especially if heading through colder states. Layers, warm jackets, hats, and gloves are essential for comfort. If you're driving through snowy areas, it's also a good idea to make sure your car is winter-ready, with proper tires and an emergency kit.

While winter lacks the big festivals and events of other seasons, it offers a peaceful, reflective journey. The towns are quieter, and the road is often empty, giving you a sense of solitude that is rare during the rest of the year. You can enjoy the iconic Route 66 landmarks without the crowds and take your time soaking in the history.

Crowds are almost non-existent in winter, and prices drop significantly, making this the most affordable time to travel. Hotels and motels are usually available without reservations, and you can often score great deals on accommodations.

Winter is best for travelers looking for a quiet, low-cost experience and who don't mind the colder weather. Compared to summer or autumn, winter offers solitude and savings, but it also requires more preparation and flexibility, especially in terms of weather conditions.

Each season along Route 66 offers a different experience, from the lively and hot summer months to the quiet, snow-dusted winter. Whether you're seeking adventure, beautiful landscapes, or a peaceful retreat, Route 66 has something to offer all year round. By considering the climate, activities, and your own preferences, you can choose the perfect time to embark on your Route 66 journey.

Duration of your trip

The duration of your trip along Route 66 can vary greatly depending on how much time you want to spend exploring the many sights, towns, and attractions along the way. Route 66 stretches for about 2,448 miles from Chicago to Santa Monica, and how long it takes to drive this iconic route depends on your travel style and interests.

For a fast-paced trip, some travelers manage to complete the entire journey in about two weeks. This means spending most of your time on the road, driving long distances each day with quick stops at key attractions. If you're mainly interested in seeing the famous landmarks without spending too much time in each place, two weeks can work. You'll get a good sense of the road and hit the major highlights, but it won't leave much room for in-depth exploration.

For a more relaxed and thorough experience, three to four weeks is ideal. This allows you to take your time and really dive into the charm of the small towns, meet the locals, and explore off-the-beaten-path attractions. You can spend more time in the unique roadside diners, old motels, museums, and natural wonders that make Route 66 so special. This slower pace also means less time spent driving long hours, giving you the chance to enjoy your trip without feeling rushed.

Another factor to consider is how much of Route 66 you plan to travel. Some people choose to drive the entire route from Chicago to Santa Monica, while others may focus on a specific section, such as the western half that passes through the scenic landscapes of Arizona, New Mexico, and California. If you're only doing a part of the route, a week or even just a few days could be enough, depending on how much time you have.

It's also important to think about how often you'll want to stop. Route 66 is full of quirky roadside attractions, historical sites, and beautiful landscapes, and you'll likely want to take your time to explore many of these stops. This might mean pulling over more frequently than on a typical road trip, which can make the journey longer but also more enjoyable.

In planning the duration of your trip, consider the time of year as well. Summer trips can be slower due to heavier traffic and the need for breaks in the heat, while winter trips might be quicker but require more caution, especially in snowy or icy conditions.

The duration of your Route 66 trip depends on how much time you can spare and how deeply you want to explore this historic road. If you're in a hurry, two weeks will get you through the basics. But if you have the luxury of time, taking three to four weeks will give you a richer, more memorable experience.

Route 66 on a budget

Exploring Route 66 on a budget is not only possible but can also enhance the authenticity and charm of your journey. With careful planning, you can experience the best of this historic route without breaking the bank, while still enjoying its many attractions, local flavors, and unique charm. Traveling affordably along Route 66 doesn't mean sacrificing comfort or missing out on what makes it special.

One of the best ways to maximize savings is to time your visit during the shoulder seasons, which are late spring and early fall. During these months, the weather is generally pleasant, and you avoid the peak summer crowds and prices. Hotels and motels often lower their rates, and the popular attractions are less crowded, allowing you to take in the sights more leisurely. You'll also have a better chance of finding last-minute deals on accommodations and activities. Winter can offer even greater savings, but some attractions may have shorter hours, and colder weather may require you to plan accordingly.

Finding budget-friendly accommodations along Route 66 is easier than you might think. One option is to stay in the many retro motels that dot the route. These often provide an affordable and nostalgic lodging experience, with rates ranging from $50 to $80 per night. Examples include the Blue Swallow Motel in Tucumcari, New Mexico, or the Wigwam Motel in Holbrook, Arizona, both offering a mix of affordability and character. If you're looking for something even more economical, consider hostels, budget hotels, or vacation rentals through platforms like Airbnb, where you can find rooms starting around $30 to $60 per night depending on the location. You can also save by booking in advance or staying in smaller towns just outside the more touristy areas.

When it comes to enjoying the attractions along Route 66, there are plenty of ways to keep costs low while still making the most of the experience. Many of the iconic sites, like Cadillac Ranch in Texas or the Route 66 Museum in Oklahoma, are free or have minimal entry fees. Plan your activities around the numerous roadside attractions and historical landmarks that don't cost a thing. You can also time your visit to coincide with local festivals and events, which are often free or inexpensive and provide a great way to immerse yourself in the local culture. Another cost-saving tip is to explore nature by hiking or picnicking in scenic spots along the way, such as the Petrified Forest National Park in Arizona, which offers stunning views for the price of a modest entrance fee.

Dining on a budget along Route 66 is a fun part of the adventure, as it gives you the chance to sample local diners and cafés known for their affordable, hearty meals. Many small-town diners along the route offer lunch specials or generous portions at reasonable prices. For example, you can grab a filling meal at Lou Mitchell's in Chicago or Joe & Aggie's Café in Holbrook for around $10 to $15. Another great way to save is to stock up on groceries at local markets and have picnics at some of the scenic stops along the way. If you're traveling with a group, sharing meals or ordering family-style at some of the local eateries can also help cut down costs. Food trucks or street vendors, when available, offer an affordable option to taste local specialties without overspending.

For transportation, the key is to plan ahead. While driving is the main mode of transportation on Route 66, there are ways to save on fuel. Carpooling with fellow travelers, renting a fuel-efficient vehicle, or taking advantage of gas rewards programs can reduce costs significantly. Additionally, check for discount cards or passes that might give you access to certain museums or attractions at a reduced price. Make sure your vehicle is in good condition to avoid costly repairs on the road, and consider packing some basic snacks and drinks to cut down on frequent stops at convenience stores.

Making the most of a budget-friendly trip to Route 66 is all about balancing the adventure with smart planning. By timing your visit during the shoulder seasons, opting for unique and affordable accommodations, seeking out free or low-cost activities, and savoring local cuisine without overspending, you can enjoy the full experience of Route 66 without straining your wallet. The charm of the journey lies in the unexpected discoveries, the open road, and the people you meet along the way—none of which require a lavish budget. With a little planning and flexibility, you'll find that exploring Route 66 on a budget is not only doable but incredibly rewarding.

Choosing the right tour package

Selecting the right tour package for Route 66 can greatly enhance your experience of the historic highway, offering an organized and insightful way to explore its iconic landmarks. There are several types of tour packages available, each catering to different preferences and travel styles. Whether you're looking for a fully guided experience or a more independent adventure, Route 66 has options to fit every type of traveler.

Guided tours are among the most popular for those seeking an in-depth exploration of Route 66. These tours are led by experienced guides who bring the history and culture of the route to life, often sharing stories and insights that aren't easily found in guidebooks. Guided tours typically range from five to fifteen days, depending on the package. Some of these tours include luxury buses, stops at major attractions, and accommodations along the way, such as the Route 66 Motor Tour, which covers significant stretches of the highway over 12 days with prices starting at around $2,500 per person. These packages often include meals, accommodation, entrance to attractions, and even entertainment. For travelers who prefer a stress-free journey where all the logistics are handled, guided tours are ideal.

Self-guided tours offer more flexibility for travelers who want to experience Route 66 at their own pace. These packages often provide detailed itineraries, maps, and insider tips but leave the driving and daily planning to you. With a self-guided tour, you can decide how much time to spend at each stop and choose your accommodations based on your budget and preferences. Prices for self-guided tours are often much lower, ranging from $300 to $800, depending on the inclusions like pre-booked hotels or car rentals. These tours are great for independent travelers who want structure but still enjoy the freedom to veer off the beaten path.

For more adventurous travelers, there are packages that include biking, hiking, or even vintage car rentals to drive the route in style. Adventure excursions like the Route 66 Motorcycle Tour allow you to ride along the highway on a classic Harley-Davidson, offering a thrilling and immersive way to experience the open road. These tours usually last around 10 days, with costs starting at $4,000, including bike rentals, guides, and accommodations. The sense of adventure and the open-road spirit are especially appealing to those seeking a more hands-on experience of Route 66.

When choosing a tour package, it's important to consider the type of traveler you are. For families, a guided or self-guided tour that highlights family-friendly attractions, like the Gateway Arch in St. Louis or the Albuquerque BioPark, might be more suitable. Guided tours that include activities for all ages, such as visiting historical museums and amusement parks, ensure that the trip is engaging for everyone. Couples might prefer a romantic, slower-paced tour, stopping at scenic lookouts, nostalgic motels, and charming small-town diners. Solo adventurers often enjoy self-guided or adventure tours, allowing for more personal reflection and spontaneous exploration. Group travelers, especially those celebrating a reunion or a special occasion, might find larger bus tours ideal for creating shared memories without the hassle of organizing everything themselves.

The timing of your trip is also important when selecting a tour package. Summer tends to be the most popular time for Route 66 tours, meaning there will be more tour options but also larger crowds and higher prices. Spring and fall are excellent alternatives, offering milder weather and fewer tourists. Many guided tours operate year-round but might alter their itineraries depending on the season. For example, winter tours might skip over certain attractions that close in colder weather but can offer a more peaceful and picturesque view of the route.

Local guides and past travelers often share insights into hidden gems that aren't included in every tour package. For instance, small towns like Oatman, Arizona, known for its wild burros roaming the streets, or the Blue Whale of Catoosa in Oklahoma, are often overlooked by larger tours. These places can offer a more intimate glimpse of Route 66's quirky side, and some tour operators specialize in these lesser-known spots. It's worth doing some research or asking your tour operator for suggestions if you want to experience something off the beaten path.

When booking a tour package, there are several factors to keep in mind to ensure you're getting the best value. Booking well in advance can save you money, especially if you're traveling during the peak summer months. Look for early-bird discounts or last-minute deals through online travel platforms or directly with tour operators. Always check the details of what's included in the package. Some packages may seem affordable upfront but could have hidden costs like entrance fees or meals. Reliable tour operators, such as Trafalgar or Intrepid Travel, are known for their comprehensive packages and positive customer reviews, making them a good starting point for your search.

If you prefer more flexibility, many tour operators offer customizable packages, allowing you to tailor the trip to your preferences. You can combine a guided tour for certain portions of Route 66 with self-guided segments, giving you a blend of structure and freedom. This can be particularly helpful if you want to explore certain attractions on your own but still appreciate the convenience of a guided experience for the rest of the trip.

In choosing the right tour package, it's essential to reflect on what you want to get out of your Route 66 experience. Whether you're seeking an educational journey through American history, a nostalgic trip down memory lane, or an adventurous ride through scenic landscapes, there's a tour package that can cater to your needs. Taking the time to research your options and think about your travel goals will ensure that your Route 66 adventure is one to remember.

Entry and visa requirements

When planning a trip along Route 66, it's important for international travelers to be aware of the entry and visa requirements. While Route 66 itself is entirely within the United States, the visa process depends on the traveler's nationality and their purpose for visiting. Understanding the visa requirements is crucial for ensuring a smooth entry into the U.S.

Visa requirements for entering the U.S. vary by nationality. Citizens of certain countries may be eligible to enter the U.S. under the Visa Waiver Program (VWP), which allows visitors to stay for up to 90 days without a visa. Countries participating in the VWP include most European Union nations, Japan, South Korea, Australia, and New Zealand. Travelers from these countries can apply for an Electronic System for Travel Authorization (ESTA) before departure. This is a quick, online process that typically takes only a few minutes to complete, though it's recommended to apply at least 72 hours before travel.

For travelers from countries not covered under the Visa Waiver Program, a B-2 tourist visa is usually required. This visa allows travelers to stay in the U.S. for up to six months for leisure purposes, including sightseeing and touring Route 66. To determine whether you need a visa, consult the U.S. Department of State's website, which provides a full list of visa requirements based on nationality.

The visa application process typically begins with completing the DS-160 online nonimmigrant visa application form. This form requires personal details, travel plans, and the reason for your visit. After submitting the form, you will need to schedule an appointment at the nearest U.S. embassy or consulate for an interview. Required documents include a valid passport, a recent passport-sized photograph, proof of travel arrangements, accommodation bookings, and financial documents showing that you can support yourself during your stay. If you are staying with family or friends, a letter of invitation may be required. Additionally, you should bring any previous U.S. visas or entry documents if applicable.

During the visa interview, the consular officer may ask about your travel plans, the purpose of your visit, and your ties to your home country. It's important to provide honest and consistent answers. Approval times vary, but it's advisable to apply several weeks before your intended travel date. Some countries may also require an additional background check, which can extend processing times.

To ensure a smooth visa application process, it's important to begin researching the requirements early. The U.S. visa process can take time, particularly if you need to gather supporting documents. It's recommended to use only official resources like the U.S. Department of State's website or the specific embassy site for your country to avoid misinformation. Double-check all documentation before attending your visa interview to ensure that everything is in order.

For travelers using the Visa Waiver Program, applying for ESTA well before your departure date is critical. While most applications are approved within minutes, there are rare cases where approval may be delayed or denied. If this happens, you may need to apply for a regular visa, which can take more time. It's also important to note that the ESTA approval only allows you to board a flight to the U.S.; final admission is determined by U.S. Customs and Border Protection officers upon arrival.

For example, a traveler from France visiting Route 66 would be eligible for the Visa Waiver Program. They would need to apply for an ESTA at least 72 hours before departure. If approved, they could stay in the U.S. for up to 90 days without a visa, enjoying the sights of Route 66. On the other hand, a traveler from India would need to apply for a B-2 tourist visa. After completing the DS-160 form, they would schedule an interview at the U.S. consulate, bringing with them proof of their travel arrangements, accommodation bookings, and financial documents to show they can cover the trip's expenses.

For travelers from countries with a higher visa denial rate, providing strong evidence of ties to their home country is important. This can include employment contracts, property ownership documents, or proof of family relationships. These documents help assure the consular officer that you intend to return to your home country after your visit.

In terms of timing, it's best to start the visa application process several months before your planned trip, especially during busy seasons when embassies can experience longer wait times for appointments. Travelers should also be aware of the peak summer months, when demand for visas can increase due to tourism, and plan accordingly.

When planning your Route 66 adventure, be mindful of any restrictions or recommendations from your home country regarding U.S. travel. Additionally, ensure that your passport is valid for at least six months beyond your intended stay in the U.S., as this is a requirement for entry for many nationalities.

Navigating entry and visa requirements for Route 66 is an essential part of planning your trip, but with the right preparation, it can be a smooth process. Make sure to research the specific requirements for your nationality, apply in advance, and keep all your documentation organized to ensure a worry-free journey.

Essential Tips for Travelers

Traveling along Route 66 is an exciting and unforgettable experience, but there are some essential tips to keep in mind to ensure that your journey is smooth, enjoyable, and safe.

One of the most important things to consider is your transportation. Since Route 66 spans over 2,400 miles, having a reliable vehicle is essential. Make sure your car is in good condition before starting the trip, with tires, brakes, and fluids checked. It's also a good idea to carry a spare tire, a basic tool kit, and a first aid kit, as some stretches of the road are quite remote with limited services. Renting a car is a popular option, and for an extra nostalgic touch, many travelers opt for renting a classic car or convertible to enhance the Route 66 experience.

Another important aspect is planning your route ahead of time. While much of the original Route 66 remains, some parts have been replaced by modern highways, and not all stretches are clearly marked. It's helpful to use a detailed map or a GPS that shows the historic route, or you can use specialized Route 66 guidebooks and apps that highlight key attractions, scenic stops, and recommended restaurants. Flexibility is also key. Some of the best moments on Route 66 happen when you take a detour to explore a small town or hidden gem that isn't on your itinerary.

Packing smartly is another essential tip. Depending on the season, you'll want to be prepared for varying weather conditions. Summers can be hot, especially in the Southwest, so pack light, breathable clothing, sunscreen, and plenty of water. If you're traveling in spring or fall, be ready for cooler evenings, and during the winter months, snow and ice may affect travel in some areas, so it's wise to pack warmer clothes and check weather forecasts regularly. Comfortable shoes are a must since you'll likely be walking around at many stops, from museums to scenic viewpoints.

Accommodations on Route 66 offer a range of experiences, from quirky motels and roadside inns to chain hotels and bed-and-breakfasts. Booking your stays in advance, especially during peak travel months, is recommended. However, if you prefer a more spontaneous trip, you'll still find plenty of last-minute options along the way. Some motels are historic landmarks themselves, offering a nostalgic glimpse into the past with neon signs and vintage decor. Staying at these iconic locations adds to the charm of the journey.

Budgeting for your trip is another key factor. While Route 66 can be affordable, costs can add up depending on your preferences for accommodations, dining, and activities. One way to save money is to explore local diners, which often serve delicious, home-cooked meals at lower prices than larger restaurants. Roadside attractions, many of which are free or have minimal entrance fees, also offer a budget-friendly way to enjoy the journey.

Another tip is to embrace the slower pace of travel on Route 66. This isn't a road trip for rushing from point A to point B. The joy of Route 66 is in taking your time, exploring the small towns, and meeting the friendly locals. Many of the towns along the way have unique histories and offer an authentic

American road trip experience, from vintage gas stations to quirky roadside attractions like the Cadillac Ranch or the Blue Whale of Catoosa. Stopping for a quick chat with shop owners or grabbing a bite at a local diner adds richness to your journey.

Safety should always be a priority when traveling long distances. Keep your phone charged, and if you're driving through more remote areas, make sure to have enough fuel, as gas stations can be far apart in some stretches, especially in the desert areas. It's also helpful to let someone know your itinerary or expected arrival times if you're traveling alone.

One of the most essential tips is to have fun and soak in the experience. Route 66 is more than just a road; it's a piece of American history, full of stories, legends, and diverse cultures. Take plenty of pictures, collect souvenirs, and make memories that will last a lifetime. This iconic highway offers something for everyone, whether you're a history buff, a nature lover, or simply seeking adventure on the open road.

CHAPTER 2.

GETTING TO ROUTE 66

Choosing the Best flights

When planning a trip to Route 66, selecting the best flight is an important step in ensuring a smooth and enjoyable journey. While Route 66 itself is a road trip, you will need to fly into one of the major cities near the highway's starting points to begin your adventure. Choosing the right flight involves considering a few factors such as airlines, costs, seasonal variations, and what amenities suit your needs.

Several major airlines offer direct flights to airports located near Route 66, including Chicago O'Hare International Airport, Los Angeles International Airport, and airports in cities like St. Louis, Albuquerque, and Oklahoma City, which are along the route. Airlines like American Airlines, United, Delta, and Southwest offer frequent flights to these destinations, often with multiple daily options from major hubs. Flight times will depend on your starting point, but direct flights from cities like New York or Miami to Chicago take about 3 hours, while flights to Los Angeles from the East Coast can range between 5 to 6 hours. The service offered by these airlines can vary slightly, with some offering more in-flight entertainment or better economy seating, so it's worth checking reviews if comfort is a top priority for your long flight.

When it comes to finding the best deals, flexibility is key. Flight prices tend to be lower if you book several months in advance, and mid-week flights are often cheaper than those departing on weekends. Using price comparison websites like Skyscanner or Google Flights can help you spot the best deals quickly, and setting up fare alerts will notify you when prices drop. Many airlines also run sales and promotions, especially during off-peak travel seasons, so keeping an eye on these can save you a significant amount. Being flexible with your travel dates is one of the easiest ways to get a cheaper flight.

Flight prices can also vary depending on the time of year. Summer and early fall are popular times for Route 66 travelers, so flights tend to be more expensive during these months. If you're looking to save, consider flying in the shoulder seasons, like late spring or early fall, when the weather is still pleasant, but flights and accommodations are more affordable. Winter flights can be the cheapest, but depending on your route, weather conditions on Route 66 may be less predictable, especially in the northern regions where snow is common. Booking your flights in advance during peak seasons can help you secure a better price, while last-minute deals are more common in the off-season.

It's also important to consider any airport fees, taxes, or additional charges that may be added to your ticket price. Most airports include these fees in your fare, but it's always good to double-check during the booking process. Some airlines may also charge additional fees for services like seat selection, in-flight meals, or checked baggage. To minimize these costs, pack light and make use of carry-on allowances. Many airlines offer a free carry-on bag, but checked baggage fees can range from $25 to $50 per bag depending on the airline, so being aware of baggage policies before booking can help you avoid unnecessary charges.

Speaking of baggage, each airline has its own policies regarding carry-on and checked luggage. For most major airlines, you're allowed one carry-on bag and one personal item (like a small backpack or handbag) for free. However, budget airlines or basic economy tickets may have stricter limitations, and you might be charged for even a carry-on bag. It's also worth noting that oversized or additional luggage, such as camping gear or souvenirs you pick up along Route 66, may incur extra fees, so planning ahead will help you stay within your budget.

Airlines typically offer several travel classes, from economy to first class. Economy is the most affordable option, and on short flights, it's often sufficient for most travelers. If you prefer a little more comfort, premium economy offers extra legroom and often better in-flight services, such as meals and drinks included in the price. Business and first-class tickets come with more luxurious perks like fully reclining seats, priority boarding, and access to airport lounges. Depending on the length of your flight and your budget, upgrading to premium economy or business class could be a good option, particularly if you're starting your journey with a long-haul flight from abroad.

When booking your flight, there are a few tips that can help you get the best experience. The best time to book is typically around two to three months before your departure date for domestic flights, though international flights may require more lead time to get the best prices. Be sure to check the airline's cancellation and change policies in case your plans shift. Some airlines allow you to make changes for free or for a small fee, while others might charge steep penalties. It's also a good idea to consider travel insurance, which can cover unexpected cancellations, medical emergencies, or lost luggage during your trip.

If you travel frequently, enrolling in an airline loyalty program can offer added benefits and savings. Many major airlines offer programs that let you earn miles or points on each flight, which can later be redeemed for free flights, seat upgrades, or other perks. For those planning multiple trips, this can be an easy way to rack up rewards while flying to your Route 66 destination. Some credit cards also offer bonus points or miles when you book flights with specific airlines, which can be a great way to save on future travel.

Selecting the best flight to Route 66 depends on several factors, including timing, budget, and personal preferences. By researching airlines, being flexible with travel dates, and using price comparison tools, you can find a flight that suits your needs. Whether you're looking for the best deal or extra comfort during your journey, taking the time to plan ahead will ensure you start your Route 66 adventure in the best way possible.

Route 66 airport: Arrival and Orientation

When you arrive for your Route 66 adventure, the airports near the starting points of this iconic road trip will be your first stop. Whether you land in Chicago, Los Angeles, or one of the cities along the route like St. Louis or Albuquerque, getting your bearings at the airport is an important first step.

If you're starting your journey in Chicago, you'll likely arrive at O'Hare International Airport, which is one of the busiest airports in the world. It can be a bit overwhelming, but there are plenty of signs to guide you. Once you've picked up your luggage, you can find rental car services within the airport, which is ideal for starting your road trip. There are also shuttles, trains, and taxis available if you need to reach your accommodation or explore the city before beginning your Route 66 drive. The airport is well connected to public transportation, so if you plan to spend a day or two in Chicago before hitting the road, you can easily catch a train into downtown.

For travelers starting in Los Angeles, Los Angeles International Airport (LAX) is the main hub. Like O'Hare, it's a large airport with multiple terminals, but there are clear signs and information desks to help you navigate. After arriving, you'll find rental car services at various locations near the airport. LAX offers shuttle buses to these rental centers, making it easy to pick up your vehicle and get on the road. If you prefer to take a day or two to explore Los Angeles, taxis and rideshare services are plentiful, and the airport is connected to public transport, such as buses that can take you into the heart of the city.

St. Louis Lambert International Airport is another option if you are starting your Route 66 trip from Missouri. It's smaller and easier to navigate than airports in Chicago or Los Angeles, which can make your arrival feel more relaxed. Once you land, car rental services are located directly at the airport, so you can start your journey quickly. The airport also offers public transportation options if you want to explore St. Louis before beginning your road trip. Taxis and shuttle services are readily available as well.

In Albuquerque, Albuquerque International Sunport serves as the main airport, and its southwestern architecture and décor provide a warm welcome. This airport is smaller than some of the others but just as convenient for starting your journey. After you collect your luggage, car rentals are easy to access, and there are also taxis, shuttles, and public transport options to get you around the city. Albuquerque is a great place to explore before continuing on Route 66.

Once you've arrived and gathered your luggage, orienting yourself at the airport is simple with the help of maps and airport staff. If you need directions, don't hesitate to ask at an information desk or use the airport's official app, which often has up-to-date details on services and transportation options. It's also a good idea to look out for signs that guide you to car rentals, taxis, or public transport if you're heading straight for the road.

Before you leave the airport, ensure you have everything you need for your road trip, like snacks, maps, or any essentials you couldn't bring on the flight. Some airports have convenience stores where you can pick up last-minute supplies. You might also want to download a navigation app or ensure your GPS system is ready to guide you along Route 66. If you need any travel advice, airports often have tourism information desks where you can get brochures or recommendations for the best places to visit along the route.

Starting your Route 66 trip from any of these airports is fairly straightforward, and they all offer the convenience of car rentals and good transportation connections to the city. Once you've gathered your belongings, sorted out your transport, and got a feel for the airport, you'll be ready to hit the road and begin your Route 66 adventure. Each of these airports makes it easy to start your journey in comfort, whether you decide to explore the city for a day or head straight to the highway.

Journey to Route 66

The journey to Route 66 is as exciting as the road trip itself. Whether you're flying in from another country or traveling from within the United States, preparing for this adventure involves a few key steps that will set you up for an unforgettable experience. Route 66 stretches from Chicago to Los Angeles, so you'll need to choose your starting point and plan accordingly.

If you're starting in Chicago, you'll probably arrive at O'Hare International Airport, one of the busiest in the world. The city of Chicago is full of iconic sights like the Willis Tower and Navy Pier, so it's worth spending a day or two exploring before you head west on Route 66. Chicago is the official starting point of the historic highway, marked by a sign downtown. Once you're ready, picking up a rental car is easy, with many options available right at the airport or nearby.

For those beginning their journey from Los Angeles, you'll arrive at Los Angeles International Airport (LAX). Like Chicago, Los Angeles has plenty to offer, from the beaches of Santa Monica to the glamor of Hollywood. The Route 66 sign at the Santa Monica Pier marks the end of the road for those starting in Chicago, but for travelers starting in LA, it's the gateway to adventure. Whether you decide to take in some sights or hit the road right away, LA makes for an exciting launch point.

If you're flying into St. Louis or Albuquerque to start your Route 66 trip, you'll find both cities offer a more laid-back experience compared to Chicago or LA, but they still have plenty of charm. St. Louis is known for the Gateway Arch, while Albuquerque offers a blend of Native American culture and vibrant Southwestern landscapes. Both cities make great starting points if you want to jump into the heart of the Route 66 journey rather than beginning at either end.

Once you've picked your starting point, you'll need to think about transportation. Renting a car is the most popular option, as it gives you the freedom to explore at your own pace. Classic American cars are often a fun choice for a Route 66 trip, adding a nostalgic feel to your drive. You'll find rental car options at any major airport, and it's best to book your car in advance, especially during peak travel seasons like summer. If you're planning to return your car at a different location, make sure to check for one-way rental options, as some companies may charge extra for this.

Before you hit the road, it's a good idea to stock up on essentials. Snacks, drinks, a good playlist, and a camera are must-haves for your journey. While there are plenty of gas stations and convenience stores along Route 66, having a few things ready from the start can make your drive more comfortable. Make sure your phone or GPS device is charged and ready to guide you, though part of the fun of Route 66 is getting off the beaten path and exploring without a strict schedule.

As you begin your journey, you'll quickly notice that Route 66 is more than just a highway. It's a living piece of American history, with old diners, motels, and roadside attractions dotting the landscape. From the bustling streets of Chicago to the desert expanses of Arizona, the route offers a constantly changing view of the country. Each town you pass through has its own unique character, with local landmarks and friendly people eager to share stories about the road.

The journey itself is about the freedom of the open road. There's no rush to reach your destination. In fact, Route 66 is best enjoyed slowly, with plenty of stops to soak in the sights and history along the way. You'll find quirky attractions like the Cadillac Ranch in Texas or the Blue Whale in Oklahoma, as well as classic diners where you can enjoy a slice of pie and a cup of coffee just like travelers did decades ago.

Whether you're traveling for a week or just a few days, your journey to Route 66 will leave you with memories of wide-open skies, friendly encounters, and the sense of adventure that only a road trip can offer. With a bit of planning and an open mind, you'll be ready to embrace all that this legendary highway has to offer.

Train Options

Traveling by train along Route 66 can be a unique and enjoyable experience, though it's important to note that the original highway itself was designed for cars. However, many of the cities and towns along the route are accessible by train, making it a great option for those who want to explore parts of the historic route without driving the entire way.

Amtrak is the primary train service in the United States and offers several routes that run parallel to or near portions of Route 66. The Southwest Chief is one of the most popular trains for travelers looking to experience parts of the famous highway. This route runs between Chicago and Los Angeles, stopping in cities like St. Louis, Albuquerque, and Flagstaff, which are all key points along Route 66. The train ride takes you through the American Midwest, deserts, and mountains, offering some stunning views of the countryside.

If you're planning to use the train to explore Route 66, you can mix your trip with both train rides and short car rentals at different points. For example, you could start your journey by taking the Southwest Chief from Chicago to Albuquerque and rent a car from there to drive through parts of New Mexico and Arizona, where Route 66 history is rich. This option allows you to enjoy the relaxing experience of train travel and still get the full Route 66 road trip vibe.

One of the benefits of taking the train is that you can enjoy the journey without the stress of driving. You'll have time to relax, take in the scenery, and meet fellow travelers. Amtrak offers different seating options, from standard coach seats to private sleeper cabins if you're traveling overnight. Prices for train tickets vary depending on the season, the type of seat or cabin you choose, and how far in advance you book. Coach seats are generally affordable, and if you're looking for comfort on a longer trip, upgrading to a roomette or bedroom can make the journey even more pleasant.

Train travel along Route 66 offers a slower, more scenic approach to the trip. While you won't have the flexibility of stopping at every small roadside attraction, the train does pass through many interesting towns and landmarks. In cities like Flagstaff, you'll be able to disembark and explore areas like the Grand Canyon or other nearby attractions before continuing on your way.

When planning your trip, it's a good idea to book your train tickets in advance, especially if you're traveling during the summer or around holidays. Amtrak often offers discounts for booking early, and you can also look out for special promotions. If you're traveling as a group or with family, there are often deals available for multiple passengers.

Packing for a train trip is a bit different than packing for a road trip. Since you won't have the same kind of flexibility, it's a good idea to bring snacks, entertainment, and anything you might need to keep comfortable during the ride. Amtrak trains do have dining cars, so you can purchase meals and snacks on board, but having your own food can save you money.

In addition to the Southwest Chief, other regional trains can get you close to parts of Route 66. For instance, the Texas

Eagle runs between Chicago and San Antonio, with stops in St. Louis, offering another option for those wanting to explore that section of the route. You can combine various train routes to create a customized journey that follows much of the historic highway's path.

Using trains to explore Route 66 offers a unique perspective on the classic American road trip. While it's not a replacement for driving the entire route, it's a great way to experience many of the route's highlights, especially for those who prefer not to drive long distances. The combination of scenic train rides and road trip stops makes for a memorable and relaxing journey across the heart of the United States.

Bus Option

Traveling along Route 66 by bus is a convenient and affordable option for many travelers. While the famous highway was primarily designed for cars, several bus companies offer services that can take you to various towns and attractions along the route. This can be a great way to explore the historic road without the need to drive.

Greyhound is the most well-known bus service in the United States, and it operates several routes that connect to cities along Route 66. You can catch a bus from major cities like Chicago, Los Angeles, and many others, stopping in key locations such as St. Louis, Oklahoma City, Amarillo, and Flagstaff. The buses are generally comfortable, with options for different seating classes, allowing you to choose what best suits your needs and budget.

One of the advantages of traveling by bus is that it can be very budget-friendly. Tickets are usually cheaper than train fares or flying, making it an ideal option for travelers looking to save money. It's a good idea to book your tickets in advance, especially if you're planning to travel during busy seasons like summer or around holidays, as prices can go up the closer you get to your departure date.

The bus rides can vary in duration depending on your route, so it's essential to check the schedules and plan accordingly. Some trips may take longer than others, especially if there are multiple stops along the way. However, the journey itself can be quite scenic, allowing you to enjoy the landscapes of the

American Southwest as you travel through deserts, mountains, and small towns.

When traveling by bus, it's important to be prepared for the ride. Bring along snacks and drinks, as food options on the bus may be limited. Many bus services allow you to carry a small bag with personal items, which can include books, games, or anything else to keep you entertained during the trip. Charging ports are available on many modern buses, so you can keep your devices powered up.

Once you arrive at your destination, you'll find that many bus stations are located near downtown areas or close to popular attractions, making it easier to explore the local sights. From there, you can either walk to nearby attractions or use local public transport, like buses or trams, to get around. In larger cities, rideshare services are also an option.

If you're looking to explore different parts of Route 66, consider creating an itinerary that includes various stops along the way. For example, you can travel from Chicago to St. Louis, enjoy the sights there, and then continue on to Tulsa or Oklahoma City. Each town has its unique charm and offers various attractions related to the Route 66 experience.

There are also smaller regional bus companies that operate in specific areas along Route 66. These companies may provide more localized service, allowing you to reach smaller towns and attractions that larger bus lines might not cover. Researching these options can help you create a more customized journey.

Traveling by bus along Route 66 may require some flexibility in your schedule since buses may not run as frequently as trains or flights. However, this mode of transportation can be an adventure in itself, as you meet fellow travelers and enjoy the camaraderie that comes with sharing the journey.

Choosing to travel along Route 66 by bus can be a rewarding experience. It offers an opportunity to see the country from a different perspective, meet interesting people, and save money while exploring some of the most iconic sights in America. Whether you are a solo traveler, a couple, or a group, the bus option provides a practical way to experience the nostalgia and beauty of Route 66.

CHAPTER 3
ACCOMMODATION OPTION

Unique Stays Along Route 66

Exploring the unique stays along Route 66 is like stepping back in time while still enjoying the charm and hospitality that make the journey special. Each of these motels has a character of its own, full of stories from the golden age of road trips. If you're planning a budget-friendly trip along this iconic highway, these motels offer a mix of nostalgia, comfort, and affordability. Here are five great places to stay:

Wigwam Motels are some of the most famous lodgings along Route 66. You can find them in a few locations, but one of the most iconic is the Wigwam Motel in Holbrook, Arizona, located at 811 W Hopi Dr, Holbrook, AZ 86025. The easiest way to get there is by following Route 66 through the town of Holbrook. The motel is hard to miss with its teepee-shaped rooms that instantly take you back to the 1950s. Staying here feels like you're part of Route 66 history. Each "wigwam" is a small, cozy room, and though the amenities are simple, it's the experience of being in such a unique place that stands out. Nearby, you can visit the Petrified Forest National Park or just spend time strolling through Holbrook itself, where many stores and restaurants embrace the Route 66 theme. For travelers on a budget, this motel offers a quirky yet affordable stay, and booking directly through their website or in advance can help secure a good rate.

Another must-see stop is the Boots Court Motel, which you'll find at 107 S Garrison Ave, Carthage, MO 64836. It's a short drive off Route 66, but it's worth it for the classic 1940s architecture and the fact that you're staying where famous guests like Clark Gable once rested. The rooms have been restored to capture the feel of the time, complete with vintage radios playing old-time music. It's affordable and adds an extra layer of historical charm to your trip. From here, you can explore the quaint town of Carthage or check out the Route 66 Drive-In theater. The motel's retro vibe is perfect for those who want to immerse themselves in the history of the road without breaking the bank.

The Blue Swallow Motel is another gem, and it's located at 815 E Route 66 Blvd, Tucumcari, NM 88401. This is one of the most beloved motels along Route 66, not only for its classic neon sign but for the warm hospitality that makes you feel like you've arrived at a home away from home. Getting here is easy—just follow Route 66 through Tucumcari, and you'll see the glowing lights of the Blue Swallow welcoming you. Each room has its own garage, a holdover from the days when motor courts were popular. The interior of the rooms is lovingly decorated with vintage touches, making it a special place to stay. While in Tucumcari, you can visit the Mesalands Dinosaur Museum or spend time exploring the murals throughout the town. It's affordable, and many travelers recommend booking in advance during the busy summer season to secure the best rates.

In Gallup, New Mexico, you'll find the El Rancho Hotel at 1000 E 66 Ave, Gallup, NM 87301. This historic hotel was once a favorite among movie stars in the 1930s and 1940s. Staying at El Rancho feels like you've stepped into a Western movie set, with its grand lobby and vintage decor. Rooms range in price, but it's possible to find good deals, especially during the off-season. While staying here, you can explore Gallup's nearby Native American art galleries or take a trip to Red Rock Park for some hiking. El Rancho offers a bit more luxury than some of the motels, but it remains an affordable option for those who want a little taste of Hollywood history on their Route 66 journey.

There's Motel Safari, located at 722 E Route 66 Blvd, Tucumcari, NM 88401, not far from the Blue Swallow Motel. Motel Safari stands out for its mid-century modern design, and it's been a favorite of travelers for decades. The rooms are spacious and decorated with vintage Route 66 memorabilia. The rates are affordable, and the motel owners are known for their friendliness and helpfulness in providing tips on what to see along the way. Tucumcari itself is small, but its charm lies in the classic feel of the town, where Route 66 remains the heart of everything. After a restful night at Motel Safari, you can continue exploring Tucumcari or move on to your next Route 66 destination.

For travelers on a budget, staying at these motels is not only an affordable way to experience Route 66 but also a way to connect with the history and culture of the road. Booking in advance and traveling during the shoulder season, like spring or fall, can help you save money while still enjoying everything these unique stays have to offer. Whether you're drawn to the quirky wigwams or the classic neon-lit motels, each stay adds something special to your journey along the Mother Road.

Recommended and Budget Friendly Stay

Exploring budget-friendly options while traveling can enhance your experience without stretching your wallet too much. Whether you're planning a cozy stay in the mountains, a serene inn, or a well-appointed resort, there are plenty of great places that offer comfort, charm, and value. Here are five excellent budget-friendly options, each with its own unique atmosphere, and plenty to offer travelers.

The Penrose Bed & Breakfast, located at 250 Red Rock Rd, Sedona, AZ 86351, is a charming and scenic getaway that offers both affordability and beauty. Getting there is easy, especially if you're driving along Route 179 in Sedona. The Penrose sits right against the iconic red rock mountains, giving guests incredible views right from their rooms. It's a small bed and breakfast, which means it feels more like a home than a hotel. The rooms are comfortable and come with personalized service, including a homemade breakfast each morning. It's a perfect spot for those who want to explore Sedona's famous hiking trails, including Bell Rock and Cathedral Rock, or take a short drive into town to browse the art galleries. For travelers on a budget, booking in advance and visiting during the off-peak season (spring or fall) will help keep costs lower, allowing you to experience the beauty of Sedona without the steep prices that can sometimes accompany this popular destination.

Two Hearts Inn, located at 2118 W Edmond Rd, Edmond, OK 73003, offers a romantic yet affordable option for couples or anyone looking for a peaceful retreat. It's located just outside of Oklahoma City, making it an easy drive via US-77 N or I-35

N if you're coming from downtown. The inn is small and intimate, with beautifully decorated rooms, perfect for a relaxing getaway. Guests love the quiet atmosphere and personalized touches like breakfast served to your room, which adds to the cozy feel. While staying here, you can explore nearby Lake Arcadia for outdoor activities like fishing, hiking, or just enjoying the lakeside views. To save money, consider booking during the week, when the rates tend to be lower, and look out for special packages they might offer.

Enchantment Resort, located at 525 Boynton Canyon Rd, Sedona, AZ 86336, may sound like a luxury resort, but it offers surprisingly good value, especially if you plan ahead. Set in one of the most picturesque areas of Sedona, Enchantment Resort is surrounded by the dramatic red rocks of Boynton Canyon, making it ideal for nature lovers. You can easily drive to the resort from Sedona by following Boynton Canyon Rd, and once there, you'll find plenty of things to do, like hiking the trails around the canyon or enjoying the resort's spa services. The rooms are spacious and designed to reflect the natural beauty of the area. While this resort may seem more luxurious, there are budget-friendly ways to enjoy it. Visiting in the off-season or mid-week can save you money on accommodations, and taking advantage of the free outdoor activities like hiking or stargazing can help you get the most out of your stay without spending too much.

Grand Casino Hotel & Resort is located at 777 Grand Casino Blvd, Shawnee, OK 74804, and offers an affordable yet exciting stay for those who enjoy entertainment and leisure activities. Just off I-40, it's easy to reach by car, especially if you're traveling from Oklahoma City or Tulsa. The hotel is part of a larger complex that includes a casino, so if you're into gaming, this is a great budget option. Even if you're not a fan of gambling, the hotel offers plenty of amenities like a pool, spa, and several restaurants, all at very reasonable rates. Guests often enjoy the live entertainment offered at the casino or simply relax at the pool. For budget travelers, keeping an eye on special promotions or booking packages that include meals or credits for casino play can help stretch your travel dollars.

Lastly, Adobe Village Inn, located at 150 Canyon Circle Dr, Sedona, AZ 86351, is a charming and affordable option that offers a cozy, southwestern experience. Getting there is simple, as it's a short drive from the main Route 179 in Sedona, surrounded by stunning rock formations. The inn itself is designed with an adobe style, which gives it a traditional and warm feel. It's a perfect place to relax after a day of exploring Sedona's trails or visiting its many vortex sites. The rooms are beautifully decorated, and guests rave about the homemade breakfast and the peaceful setting. It's a great option for travelers who want a comfortable stay without the high prices that some Sedona accommodations can charge. For those on a budget, visiting in the shoulder seasons when tourism is a bit slower can help reduce rates, and looking for mid-week stays can also help save money.

For budget travelers, these accommodations offer great options without sacrificing comfort or enjoyment. Booking in advance, traveling during off-peak times, and taking advantage of special offers will help keep costs down, allowing you to enjoy more of the beautiful destinations these places have to offer. Each of these stays has its own charm, whether you're seeking quiet mountain views, a romantic inn, or a fun-filled resort experience.

CHAPTER 4

KEY DESTINATION ALONG THE ROUTE

Illinois

Illinois is a state filled with rich history, vibrant cities, and an iconic route that brings travelers from all over the world. From the towering skyscrapers of Chicago to the nostalgic stops along Route 66, Illinois offers a wide array of experiences for any traveler. Whether you're exploring museums, enjoying outdoor adventures, or immersing yourself in local culture, this guide will help you make the most of your journey.

Arriving in Illinois is fairly straightforward, especially if you're starting in Chicago, which is serviced by O'Hare International Airport, one of the busiest airports in the world. From O'Hare, the Chicago Transit Authority (CTA) offers easy transportation into the city via the Blue Line train. If you're venturing onto Route 66, renting a car is a must. Major highways and interstates make driving throughout Illinois accessible and comfortable. Departures are just as simple, with flights and interstate access making travel hassle-free.

Chicago, as the starting point of Route 66, is a perfect blend of modernity and history. The city's skyline, anchored by Willis Tower and the John Hancock Building, is awe-inspiring, but its real charm lies in the neighborhoods. Millennium Park, with the reflective Cloud Gate sculpture (often called "The Bean"), is a must-visit for any traveler. Navy Pier offers entertainment and stunning views of Lake Michigan, while The Art Institute of Chicago holds some of the world's most famous masterpieces. If you love history, the Field Museum and the Museum of Science and Industry will immerse you in knowledge.

A visit to the Illinois Route 66 Museum in Pontiac is essential for Route 66 enthusiasts. Located at 110 W Howard St, Pontiac, IL, the museum is dedicated to preserving the history of the famous highway. The museum features an array of memorabilia, from classic cars to signage, and offers stories of the people who traveled the "Mother Road." Be sure to check out the Route 66 Hall of Fame, which honors those who made significant contributions to the highway's history. This museum is a fascinating stop where you can learn about the history and folklore that shaped the journey along Route 66.

For outdoor lovers, Illinois has plenty to offer. Chicago's lakefront offers scenic biking and walking paths, where you can enjoy the views of Lake Michigan. Further inland, Starved Rock State Park is a perfect day trip from Chicago, boasting beautiful waterfalls, canyons, and hiking trails that offer spectacular views year-round. Kayaking along the Illinois River or exploring the natural beauty of Matthiessen State Park is another outdoor adventure you shouldn't miss.

Cultural experiences abound in Illinois, starting with Chicago's world-renowned theater scene. From Broadway shows to local productions, the city offers a wide range of performances. The Chicago Symphony Orchestra and the Lyric Opera of Chicago are top-notch venues for lovers of classical music. If you're visiting in the summer, try to catch a music festival like Lollapalooza or the Chicago Blues Festival, both of which showcase incredible talent.

Illinois is home to a diverse food scene, from fine dining to deep-dish pizza. In Chicago, trying the city's famous deep-dish pizza is a must, with iconic spots like Lou Malnati's and Giordano's serving up some of the best. For a more unique local experience, head to Portillo's for a Chicago-style hot dog or Italian beef sandwich. If you're traveling down Route 66, take advantage of the diners and local eateries that capture the nostalgic essence of roadside dining. Cozy Dog Drive-In in Springfield, the birthplace of the corn dog, is a fun and tasty stop.

When it comes to highlights, exploring Chicago's skyline is an unforgettable experience. Taking an architectural boat tour along the Chicago River is a great way to see the city's famous buildings from a different perspective, with expert guides sharing the history behind them. Route 66, of course, offers its own highlights, including the iconic Gemini Giant statue in Wilmington and the small-town charm of places like Lincoln and Springfield. Be sure to take your time, as there are plenty of small attractions and quirky stops along the way that make the journey even more special.

Must-see sights in Illinois include the Abraham Lincoln Presidential Library and Museum in Springfield, which offers a deep dive into the life of one of America's most beloved presidents. Springfield itself is filled with Lincoln landmarks, including his home and tomb, which are well worth visiting. Another historic must-see is the Cahokia Mounds State Historic Site, where you can explore the remnants of the largest pre-Columbian settlement north of Mexico.

For historical highlights, the city of Galena offers beautifully preserved 19th-century buildings and a glimpse into the past. Ulysses S. Grant's home is located here, adding another layer of historical significance. In Chicago, the Chicago History Museum and the Pullman National Monument offer rich insights into the city's industrial and social history.

Guided tours are plentiful in Illinois, especially in Chicago. Walking tours, such as the Chicago Architecture Center tours, provide detailed explorations of the city's famous buildings. History buffs will enjoy the guided tours at Lincoln's Home in Springfield or a visit to Route 66 with local experts who share the stories behind the road's creation and development.

Educational opportunities abound in the city's many museums and cultural institutions, providing a deeper understanding of everything from art to science to history.

Illinois has a wealth of experiences for every traveler, from the bustling streets of Chicago to the quiet charm of Route 66's small towns. Whether you're looking to dive into the rich history, indulge in culinary delights, or enjoy outdoor activities, Illinois offers something for everyone. Planning your visit around the top attractions and must-see sights will ensure a memorable journey, and if you take the time to explore the smaller, lesser-known stops along Route 66, you'll experience the true heart of this iconic road.

Missouri

Missouri is often referred to as the "Gateway to the West," a state steeped in history, culture, and natural beauty. Whether you're venturing into the bustling city of St. Louis or exploring the nostalgic charm of Route 66 State Park, Missouri offers a blend of urban excitement and serene landscapes. This guide will take you through some of the most important things travelers should explore and do, giving you a rich and immersive experience in the heart of America.

Arriving in Missouri is relatively easy, especially if your first stop is St. Louis. Lambert-St. Louis International Airport is well connected to major cities, making it a convenient entry point for travelers. Once you've arrived, getting around the city is simple with its well-structured MetroLink light rail and MetroBus systems. If you're planning to explore the surrounding areas or travel along Route 66, renting a car is recommended for more flexibility and ease of access. Departures are equally seamless, with plenty of transportation options to help you move on to your next destination or return home.

St. Louis, the largest city in Missouri, is where the iconic Gateway Arch stands tall, symbolizing the city's role in westward expansion. The Gateway Arch National Park is a must-see for any visitor, where you can ride to the top of the arch for breathtaking views of the city and the Mississippi River. Nearby, the Old Courthouse offers a glimpse into the city's historical role in the landmark Dred Scott case. Forest Park, larger than New York's Central Park, is home to world-class attractions like the St. Louis Zoo, the St. Louis Art

Museum, and the Missouri History Museum, all of which offer free admission.

If you're drawn to outdoor adventures, Missouri has plenty to offer. Route 66 State Park, located near Eureka, is a perfect stop for those tracing the historic highway. The park offers hiking trails, picnic spots, and a visitor center that tells the story of the once-thriving communities along the "Mother Road." For those who love water-based activities, the nearby Meramec River offers excellent canoeing and fishing opportunities. In St. Louis, a walk along the Mississippi Riverfront is a great way to enjoy the city's natural beauty while soaking in its rich history.

Missouri is known for its cultural experiences, especially in St. Louis. The city boasts a thriving music scene, especially for jazz and blues, with famous venues like the National Blues Museum and BB's Jazz, Blues, and Soups offering live performances regularly. The St. Louis Symphony, located at Powell Hall, is a treat for lovers of classical music. For a unique experience, visit the City Museum, a one-of-a-kind interactive museum that's part art installation, part playground. It's fun for visitors of all ages and offers a truly memorable experience.

When it comes to dining, Missouri has a little bit of everything, but St. Louis is particularly famous for its unique take on pizza. St. Louis-style pizza, featuring a thin, cracker-like crust and Provel cheese, is a local favorite, and you can sample it at iconic spots like Imo's Pizza. For barbecue lovers, St. Louis-style ribs are a must-try, with restaurants like

Pappy's Smokehouse offering some of the best slow-smoked meats in the city. If you're traveling through small towns along Route 66, you'll find plenty of roadside diners offering traditional American comfort food, perfect for a quick and hearty meal during your journey.

Among the highlights of Missouri is, of course, the Gateway Arch, which dominates the St. Louis skyline and offers incredible views from the top. Another highlight is the Missouri Botanical Garden, one of the oldest in the country, where visitors can explore beautiful gardens, historic structures, and seasonal events. In Route 66 State Park, the preserved segments of the original Route 66 offer a nostalgic look back at a time when the highway was the main route for cross-country travelers. The park's visitor center is filled with memorabilia and photos that take you back to the golden age of road travel.

Missouri offers plenty of must-see sights and tours for travelers. In St. Louis, the Anheuser-Busch Brewery Tour is a popular stop, offering guided tours through one of the largest breweries in the world. For history buffs, the Lewis & Clark Historic Site, just across the river in Illinois, provides a detailed look at the explorers' historic journey west. Another must-see is the Ulysses S. Grant National Historic Site, where you can tour the home of the famous Civil War general and president.

Missouri is rich in historical highlights, and nowhere is this more evident than along Route 66. Small towns like Cuba and Lebanon are filled with Route 66 nostalgia, where travelers can explore vintage motels, classic diners, and restored gas stations. In St. Louis, the Missouri History Museum offers an in-depth look at the state's past, including exhibits on the 1904 World's Fair and Charles Lindbergh's historic flight across the Atlantic. For those interested in civil rights history, the Dred Scott case exhibits at the Old Courthouse are a poignant reminder of the struggles for freedom and equality.

Guided tours and educational opportunities abound in Missouri. In St. Louis, you can take an architectural walking tour to learn more about the city's historic buildings and landmarks. For those interested in nature and geology, Meramec Caverns, just outside of St. Louis, offers guided tours through its vast and beautiful underground caves. These tours provide fascinating insights into Missouri's natural history and make for a unique adventure. Route 66 also offers guided driving tours, where experts provide detailed commentary on the history and significance of the road and its landmarks.

Missouri's combination of urban and natural attractions offers something for everyone. St. Louis is a vibrant city that blends history, culture, and modern entertainment, while Route 66 State Park captures the essence of a bygone era. Whether you're walking along the Mississippi River, exploring the museums, or retracing the steps of America's early pioneers, Missouri promises a rich and rewarding experience. Planning your trip around these top attractions, must-see sights, and unique tours will ensure you leave the state with unforgettable memories.

Kansas

Kansas, though often known for its vast open plains, holds a special place in the heart of Route 66 travelers. Stretching for just 13 miles through the southeastern part of the state, this small segment of the Mother Road is packed with charm, history, and attractions that make it worth exploring. Galena and Baxter Springs are two of the notable towns in this area, each offering unique experiences for travelers tracing the historic highway. This guide will provide you with a comprehensive look at what to do and see while passing through these towns, along with tips to make your journey smooth and enjoyable.

Arriving in Kansas along Route 66 is a straightforward and pleasant experience. If you're traveling from Missouri, Galena will be your first stop. The nearest major airport is Joplin Regional Airport in Missouri, just a short drive away, which makes it convenient for air travelers. Driving is the most popular way to explore Route 66, so having a car is essential to fully experience the towns and attractions along the way. Baxter Springs is just a 15-minute drive southwest of Galena, making it an easy addition to your travel itinerary. When it's time to depart, you can continue your Route 66 journey westward toward Oklahoma or loop back to Missouri for further exploration.

Galena, a former mining town, is steeped in history and full of quirky roadside attractions. One of the main highlights here is Cars on the Route, a restored gas station turned gift shop that pays homage to the animated movie Cars. The shop features a tow truck named "Tow Tater," which inspired the character "Tow Mater" in the film, making it a popular photo stop.

Another key attraction is the Galena Mining & Historical Museum, where you can learn about the town's mining past and its role in the development of the area. Baxter Springs offers its own unique charm, with the Baxter Springs Heritage Center & Museum, which chronicles the town's significance during the Civil War and its Route 66 history.

Outdoor enthusiasts will find some enjoyable activities in the Kansas stretch of Route 66. The towns themselves are surrounded by beautiful open countryside, perfect for a scenic drive or a quiet moment of reflection. If you're visiting in the fall, the changing colors of the leaves add a picturesque backdrop to your journey. For those looking to stretch their legs, a walk through the historic downtown areas of both Galena and Baxter Springs offers a chance to take in the architecture and the nostalgic atmosphere of the towns. Riverside Park in Baxter Springs is a peaceful spot for a picnic, with views of the Spring River.

Cultural experiences in this part of Kansas center around its rich history. In Galena, the Main Street area offers a look at the town's past with beautifully preserved buildings and classic small-town charm. The Route 66-themed shops and restaurants give travelers a sense of stepping back in time to the heyday of the Mother Road. In Baxter Springs, the historic downtown is full of reminders of the town's significance during the Civil War, and visitors can see historic markers and monuments throughout the area. The Baxter Springs Civil War Battlefield and Cemetery is a sobering but important site to visit for those interested in American history.

Dining in this part of Kansas offers simple yet satisfying fare. In Galena, you can find casual diners and small cafes that serve classic American comfort food. One local favorite is The Front Street Diner, where you can grab a burger and a slice of pie after a long drive. In Baxter Springs, Cafe on the Route is a must-stop for anyone traveling Route 66. The menu offers a mix of traditional American dishes with a touch of local flavor, and the nostalgic decor gives the place an authentic, old-school feel. For those looking for budget-friendly options, these diners offer affordable meals that will keep you fueled for your journey.

Among the highlights of Kansas along Route 66 is the chance to experience a slice of Americana. The small towns, vintage signs, and restored gas stations offer a glimpse into the past, making the Kansas stretch feel like a living time capsule. Cars on the Route is a standout attraction, especially for fans of the movie Cars, but it's also a great place to buy souvenirs and take photos. Baxter Springs' Civil War history provides a different kind of highlight, giving travelers a chance to reflect on the town's past while also enjoying the historic Route 66 experience.

There's no shortage of things to do along Kansas' brief stretch of Route 66. In Galena, walking tours of the historic downtown area are available, and local guides can offer insights into the town's mining history and its connection to Route 66. In Baxter Springs, you can take a self-guided driving tour that takes you through key Civil War sites, as well as historic Route 66 landmarks. Don't miss the Baxter Springs Independent Oil and Gas Service Station, one of the few remaining full-service stations along the Mother Road, which has been beautifully restored.

Historical highlights in Kansas include the Galena Mining & Historical Museum, which offers a deep dive into the town's roots as a lead mining community. The museum's collection of artifacts, photos, and mining equipment helps visitors understand the town's development and its significance during the height of the mining industry. In Baxter Springs, the Heritage Center & Museum covers everything from the town's Route 66 legacy to its role in the Civil War. The museum also includes exhibits on Native American history in the region, adding an extra layer of cultural depth to your visit.

For those interested in guided tours and educational opportunities, Kansas has a few options. In Galena, you can take guided walking tours that focus on both the town's mining history and its Route 66 heritage. These tours are often led by local historians who provide fascinating anecdotes and insights that you wouldn't get by just wandering around on your own. In Baxter Springs, the guided tours at the Heritage Center & Museum cover the town's unique history, with special emphasis on its Civil War past and its time as a key stop on Route 66.

Though small, the Kansas stretch of Route 66 is packed with memorable experiences, from quirky roadside attractions to important historical sites. Galena and Baxter Springs offer a unique glimpse into the past, with their preserved landmarks and welcoming small-town feel. Whether you're a history buff, a Route 66 enthusiast, or just looking for an off-the-beaten-path adventure, Kansas offers a rewarding stop along your journey. Taking the time to explore these towns will give you a richer understanding of the region and make your Route 66 trip even more special.

Oklahoma

Oklahoma's stretch of Route 66 is one of the most celebrated and diverse portions of the historic highway, offering a mix of urban culture, nostalgic roadside attractions, and scenic landscapes. Tulsa, in particular, stands out as a vibrant city along the route, blending modern amenities with rich history. The Route 66 Historical District in Tulsa is a must-see for those tracing the Mother Road, and the area offers plenty of activities to fill your days, from exploring museums to enjoying local food. This guide will help you make the most of your journey through Oklahoma, highlighting key attractions, outdoor activities, cultural experiences, and more.

Tulsa is a central hub for travelers on Route 66, making it easy to access by both air and car. If you're flying, the Tulsa International Airport is the best option, with connections to major U.S. cities. From the airport, it's just a short drive to downtown Tulsa, where Route 66 winds through the heart of the city. For those driving, Route 66 is well-marked throughout Oklahoma, and Tulsa's location makes it an ideal stopping point. Departure from Tulsa can take you further west along Route 66 toward Oklahoma City or east toward Missouri, depending on your travel plans.

Tulsa is packed with attractions, especially for those interested in the history of Route 66. The Route 66 Historical District is the centerpiece of any visit, where you'll find the Cyrus Avery Centennial Plaza. Known as the "Father of Route 66," Cyrus Avery played a key role in creating the highway, and the plaza commemorates his legacy with sculptures, historical markers, and great views of the city. Nearby, the Blue Dome District offers a funky blend of art, culture, and nightlife, and you can't miss the famous Meadow Gold Sign, a neon icon of the Route 66 era that has been beautifully restored.

For outdoor enthusiasts, Tulsa offers plenty of opportunities to enjoy nature. The River Parks Trail system runs alongside the Arkansas River and is perfect for walking, cycling, or simply relaxing by the water. If you're looking for something more adventurous, Turkey Mountain Urban Wilderness is a short drive from downtown and provides hiking and biking trails with scenic views of the city. On a sunny day, the trails are peaceful and not too crowded, making it a great spot to reconnect with nature after spending time in the city.

Tulsa's cultural scene is lively and diverse, making it a highlight for travelers who want to dive into local experiences.

The Philbrook Museum of Art is one of the city's gems, housed in a stunning villa with beautiful gardens. Inside, you'll find a world-class collection of art ranging from Renaissance pieces to contemporary works. For something more tied to local culture, the Woody Guthrie Center celebrates the life and music of the Oklahoma-born folk singer, with exhibits that explore his influence on American music. The Greenwood District, often referred to as "Black Wall Street," is another must-visit area, with a powerful history and a vibrant community.

Tulsa's dining scene has something for everyone, from fine dining to casual eats. If you want a classic Route 66 experience, stop by Tally's Good Food Cafe, a diner famous for its hearty breakfasts and vintage vibe. For a more upscale meal, Juniper offers farm-to-table dining with a creative menu that changes with the seasons. If you're looking for local barbecue, Burn Co BBQ is a favorite among locals and visitors alike. Travelers on a budget will find plenty of affordable options, including taco trucks and sandwich shops scattered throughout the city.

A highlight of any Route 66 journey through Oklahoma is the opportunity to immerse yourself in both modern and historic attractions. Tulsa's Route 66 Historical District is one of the top highlights, offering a mix of landmarks, neon signs, and restored buildings that capture the spirit of the highway. The Circle Cinema, Tulsa's oldest operating movie theater, shows independent and classic films, and it's a great spot to take in some local culture while resting from your road trip. The Tulsa

Art Deco Museum offers a glimpse into the city's architectural history, showcasing the glamour of the 1920s and '30s.

There are many things to do in Tulsa and the surrounding areas to make your Route 66 trip memorable. Besides visiting the historic Route 66 landmarks, take a ride down the road to explore some unique roadside attractions. In nearby Catoosa, the Blue Whale of Catoosa is a whimsical stop, offering a chance to stretch your legs and take fun photos. If you're traveling with kids, they'll love this quirky landmark. Another must-see is the Oklahoma Route 66 Museum in Clinton, a short drive outside Tulsa. It offers interactive exhibits that tell the story of Route 66 from its inception to its modern-day revival.

Oklahoma's historical legacy shines through in the many museums and landmarks that dot the Route 66 corridor. One of the most important historical highlights is the Greenwood Cultural Center, which preserves the memory of the 1921 Tulsa Race Massacre and the legacy of Black Wall Street. This site is crucial for understanding Tulsa's complex history and offers educational exhibits and programs. For Route 66 enthusiasts, the Sapulpa Historical Museum is another great stop, providing insights into the history of the area and its connection to the iconic highway.

If you're interested in guided tours and educational opportunities, Tulsa offers several options. The Route 66 Interpretive Center in Chandler is just a short drive from Tulsa and provides guided tours that walk you through the history of the road. The Tulsa Historical Society & Museum also offers guided tours of the city's key historical sites, including its Art Deco architecture, oil boom history, and Route 66 connections. For those wanting to learn more about the area's Native American history, the Gilcrease Museum offers educational exhibits and tours on Native American art and history.

Tulsa and Oklahoma's Route 66 corridor provide a mix of modern attractions and historic charm that make this part of the journey unique. Whether you're exploring the vibrant downtown area, tracing the steps of history in the Greenwood District, or marveling at quirky roadside attractions, there's always something new to discover. This guide provides just a glimpse into the experiences awaiting you on your Route 66 trip through Oklahoma, offering the perfect balance of history, culture, and adventure.

Texas

Texas is an unforgettable part of any Route 66 journey, with Amarillo standing out as a key stop along the way. Famous for its larger-than-life attractions, the stretch through Texas offers a glimpse into the quirky, vast landscapes that have come to define this part of the U.S. The open plains, endless skies, and iconic stops like Cadillac Ranch create a unique atmosphere that makes the drive through Texas both fascinating and memorable. Amarillo serves as the heart of Route 66 in this area, offering a mix of art, history, and Texan charm.

For those arriving in Amarillo, the easiest way is by car along Route 66 itself, as the road is well-marked and easy to navigate. If you're flying, the Rick Husband Amarillo International Airport is located just outside the city, providing convenient access to Route 66. From there, it's a short drive to downtown Amarillo, where Route 66 runs through the Historic District. If you're continuing your journey west, you'll follow the highway toward New Mexico, or east, back into Oklahoma.

Amarillo is filled with attractions, but one of the must-see stops is Cadillac Ranch. This iconic art installation features ten half-buried Cadillacs, each spray-painted in bright colors by visitors. Located just off I-40, Cadillac Ranch is a short drive from downtown Amarillo and is a popular photo stop for travelers. It's not only a fun and quirky roadside attraction, but also an evolving piece of art, as visitors are encouraged to add their own spray paint designs to the cars. Be sure to bring a can of spray paint and leave your mark on this Route 66 classic.

For outdoor activities, Palo Duro Canyon State Park is a fantastic destination, often referred to as the "Grand Canyon of Texas." Located about 30 minutes south of Amarillo, this breathtaking canyon offers hiking, biking, and horseback riding opportunities through stunning red rock landscapes. The Lighthouse Trail is one of the most popular hikes, leading to a towering rock formation with panoramic views of the canyon. Whether you're looking for a peaceful nature escape or an adventurous trek, Palo Duro Canyon is a must-visit for outdoor lovers.

Cultural experiences in Amarillo are rooted in both the history of Route 66 and the Texan spirit. The Historic Route 66 District in downtown Amarillo is a great place to start, where you'll find antique shops, art galleries, and local boutiques housed in buildings that date back to the 1920s. The area is known for its retro charm and makes for a great walk, with plenty of Route 66 memorabilia to admire. Another cultural gem is the Amarillo Museum of Art, which showcases a variety of works from Asian art to modern American pieces, providing a peaceful and reflective space within the city.

When it comes to dining, Amarillo offers a true taste of Texas, especially if you're a fan of hearty meals and barbecue. A visit to The Big Texan Steak Ranch is almost a rite of passage for Route 66 travelers. Famous for its 72-ounce steak challenge, this iconic restaurant is an experience in itself, with its cowboy-themed decor and lively atmosphere. If you're not up for the challenge, the regular-sized steaks are just as delicious, and the restaurant often features live country music, adding to the authentic Texas vibe. For those looking for something more casual, Coyote Bluff Cafe is a local favorite known for its burgers, especially the "Burger from Hell" if you're feeling adventurous.

Amarillo is filled with highlights, and Cadillac Ranch certainly tops the list for its unique artistic flair. Another highlight is the Jack Sisemore Traveland RV Museum, which offers a nostalgic trip back in time with its collection of vintage RVs and motorcycles. For car enthusiasts or anyone curious about the early days of road travel, this museum is a fun stop that captures the spirit of the open road.

One of the top things to do in Amarillo is to simply explore the Historic Route 66 District. With its blend of historic architecture and quirky shops, it's a great place to spend an afternoon browsing through antiques, local crafts, and unique souvenirs. If you're visiting in the evening, the district's neon signs light up, giving the area a classic Route 66 feel that's hard to resist. Another must-see sight is the Don Harrington Discovery Center, especially if you're traveling with kids. This interactive science museum offers hands-on exhibits that are both fun and educational.

For those interested in historical highlights and excursions, the Panhandle-Plains Historical Museum in nearby Canyon, Texas, offers a deep dive into the history of the Texas Panhandle, from its Native American roots to the oil boom. This museum is one of the largest in the state and features exhibits on everything from geology to fine art. It's a fascinating stop for history buffs and provides an excellent overview of the region's development.

Guided tours are available for those who want a deeper understanding of the area. At Cadillac Ranch, some local guides offer historical insights into the creation of this unique landmark and its connection to the counterculture movement of the 1970s. Additionally, Palo Duro Canyon State Park offers ranger-led tours that explore the flora, fauna, and history of the canyon, making it a great way to learn more about the natural beauty of the region while enjoying the outdoors.

Amarillo and its surroundings offer a variety of educational opportunities for visitors of all ages. The Wildcat Bluff Nature Center provides guided nature walks and educational programs focused on the local ecosystem, perfect for families or anyone interested in Texas wildlife. The American Quarter

Horse Hall of Fame & Museum is another educational stop, celebrating the history and impact of this famous horse breed in the American West.

Amarillo and Cadillac Ranch are essential stops on any Route 66 adventure through Texas. With its mix of artistic attractions, historical sites, and outdoor beauty, this part of the journey offers a well-rounded experience for every type of traveler. Whether you're spray-painting Cadillacs, hiking through red rock canyons, or enjoying a classic Texas steak, the area has a little something for everyone, making it one of the most memorable stretches of the Mother Road.

New Mexico

Santa Fe and Albuquerque offer a fascinating blend of Southwestern charm, history, and culture, making them standout destinations along Route 66 in New Mexico. Santa Fe, known for its artistic community and adobe architecture, invites visitors to immerse themselves in its rich history and creative spirit. Albuquerque, on the other hand, is a sprawling city that combines modernity with Route 66 nostalgia, providing travelers with a diverse range of attractions and experiences. Together, these cities offer a unique slice of the American Southwest.

Arriving in Albuquerque is convenient, as the Albuquerque International Sunport (ABQ) serves as a major hub for flights into the region. Once you land, it's easy to rent a car and begin your journey along Route 66. If you're arriving by car from neighboring states, Interstate 40, which runs parallel to the historic Route 66, will bring you right into the heart of the city. From Albuquerque, Santa Fe is only about an hour's drive north on Interstate 25, making it an easy addition to your itinerary.

Albuquerque's stretch of Route 66 is one of the most iconic parts of the Mother Road. One of the top attractions here is the Route 66 Diner, a retro eatery that captures the spirit of the 1950s with neon signs, vintage decor, and classic American dishes. It's a must-visit for anyone exploring the area. Another popular attraction is the KiMo Theatre, a historic art deco building that still hosts performances and movie screenings. The theater's unique Pueblo Deco style combines Native

American motifs with Art Deco design, making it a visual highlight in the city.

For outdoor enthusiasts, the Sandia Mountains offer stunning hiking trails just outside Albuquerque. You can either hike up the La Luz Trail for breathtaking views of the city or take the Sandia Peak Tramway, one of the longest aerial tramways in the world, to the top. Once there, the panoramic views of the Rio Grande Valley are absolutely spectacular, especially at sunset. For a more leisurely outdoor experience, the Rio Grande Nature Center State Park offers walking trails along the river, where you can observe local wildlife and enjoy the tranquility of the natural surroundings.

Cultural experiences abound in both cities. In Albuquerque, the Indian Pueblo Cultural Center provides a deep dive into the history and culture of New Mexico's Pueblo people, featuring exhibits, traditional dances, and art displays. It's a great way to gain a better understanding of the region's indigenous heritage. In Santa Fe, the Georgia O'Keeffe Museum is a must-see for art lovers. This museum is dedicated to the work of one of America's most famous artists, whose paintings were inspired by the landscapes of New Mexico. Santa Fe's Canyon Road is another cultural highlight, home to more than 100 galleries and studios showcasing everything from contemporary art to Native American pottery.

Dining in Albuquerque and Santa Fe is a highlight of any trip, as both cities are known for their unique Southwestern cuisine. In Albuquerque, try El Pinto for some authentic New Mexican dishes, including their famous red and green chile enchiladas. If you're in the mood for something lighter, The Grove Cafe & Market offers fresh, locally sourced ingredients in a cozy setting. In Santa Fe, The Shed is a beloved spot that serves up traditional New Mexican fare, including blue corn tortillas and chile-smothered dishes. For a more upscale dining experience, Geronimo on Canyon Road offers an inventive menu in a historic adobe building, perfect for a special night out.

In terms of highlights, the Old Town Albuquerque area is a must-see. This historic district dates back to the city's founding in 1706 and is filled with charming adobe buildings, shops, galleries, and restaurants. The San Felipe de Neri Church, a beautifully preserved colonial-era church, is the centerpiece of Old Town. Take your time exploring the plaza, browsing the local crafts, and soaking in the atmosphere of this historic part of the city.

Another top thing to do in Albuquerque is to visit the Albuquerque International Balloon Fiesta if you're there in October. This world-renowned event features hundreds of hot air balloons taking to the skies, creating a colorful spectacle that attracts visitors from all over the world. Even if you're not visiting during the festival, the Anderson-Abruzzo Albuquerque International Balloon Museum provides a fascinating look into the history of ballooning.

Santa Fe's must-see sights include the Loretto Chapel, famous for its mysterious spiral staircase, and the Santa Fe Plaza, the historic heart of the city. The plaza is surrounded by shops, galleries, and the Palace of the Governors, the oldest continuously occupied public building in the United States. Just walking around the plaza and taking in the local architecture and culture is a great way to spend an afternoon.

For history buffs, the Petroglyph National Monument in Albuquerque is an intriguing site that preserves thousands of ancient rock carvings created by indigenous peoples. You can hike along several trails to view the petroglyphs, some of which are over 400 years old. In Santa Fe, the Museum of International Folk Art offers a fascinating look at folk art traditions from around the world, while the New Mexico History Museum provides insight into the state's rich and complex past.

Guided tours are a great way to learn more about the area's history and culture. In Santa Fe, walking tours of the historic downtown are available, taking you to important landmarks like the Cathedral Basilica of St. Francis of Assisi and the Palace of the Governors. In Albuquerque, you can join a guided tour of Old Town or take a ghost tour that delves into the spooky legends and haunted sites of the area.

Both cities offer numerous educational opportunities, from art workshops in Santa Fe to indigenous cultural programs in Albuquerque. The Indian Pueblo Cultural Center often hosts pottery-making demonstrations and other hands-on activities that allow visitors to connect with Native American traditions in a meaningful way. Similarly, the Santa Fe School of Cooking offers classes where you can learn to prepare traditional New Mexican dishes, making it a fun and delicious educational experience.

Santa Fe and Albuquerque are two of the most captivating stops along Route 66. With their rich history, vibrant art scenes, and stunning natural beauty, these cities offer travelers a chance to explore the heart and soul of the American Southwest. From hiking in the mountains to wandering through art galleries and sampling mouthwatering local cuisine, there's something for everyone to enjoy in this part of New Mexico. Whether you're an outdoor adventurer, a history buff, or an art lover, the combination of Santa Fe and Albuquerque will make your Route 66 journey all the more memorable.

Arizona

Arizona is a land of breathtaking landscapes and rich history, with Winslow and the Grand Canyon as two key highlights along Route 66. Winslow, famous for its connection to the Eagles' song "Take It Easy," offers a nostalgic stop on the route, while the Grand Canyon is one of the most iconic natural wonders in the world, drawing millions of visitors every year. Together, they make for an unforgettable exploration of Arizona's diverse beauty and heritage.

Arriving in Winslow is relatively simple, especially if you're traveling along Route 66. The town is easily accessible by car from Interstate 40, which runs parallel to the historic route. Winslow's small-town charm makes it a great place to stretch your legs before heading to the nearby natural wonders. If you're coming from afar, Flagstaff Pulliam Airport is the nearest major airport, located about an hour's drive west of Winslow. From here, you can rent a car and begin your journey along Route 66. The Grand Canyon is a bit farther out, roughly a 90-minute drive from Flagstaff, but it's well worth the trip.

In Winslow, the first thing travelers should do is stop by the Standin' on the Corner Park, a small but famous park inspired by the Eagles' song. A statue of a man standing with his guitar makes for a great photo opportunity, and the park captures the essence of Route 66 nostalgia. Winslow is also home to the La Posada Hotel, a beautifully restored railway hotel designed by architect Mary Colter. Even if you're not staying overnight, it's worth stopping by to admire the historic building and its gardens.

The Meteor Crater, located about 20 miles west of Winslow, is another must-see attraction. This massive, well-preserved meteorite impact site offers an awe-inspiring look at the power of nature. The visitor center provides educational exhibits and observation points for a panoramic view of the crater. You can spend an hour or so exploring this fascinating geological site before continuing your journey.

Of course, no trip to Arizona is complete without a visit to the Grand Canyon. Whether you're seeing it for the first time or the hundredth, the sheer magnitude of this natural wonder never fails to impress. The South Rim of the Grand Canyon is the most accessible area for visitors and offers numerous lookout points, including Mather Point, which provides a stunning panoramic view of the canyon. For a more immersive experience, take the Rim Trail, an easy walk along the edge of the canyon with various scenic overlooks.

For the more adventurous traveler, hiking into the Grand Canyon is an unforgettable experience. The Bright Angel Trail is one of the most popular hikes, offering stunning views as it descends into the canyon. If you're up for a longer trek, the South Kaibab Trail leads to the Colorado River, though it's best suited for experienced hikers. Mule rides along the canyon's trails are also available, providing a unique way to experience the dramatic landscapes without having to hike the steep paths yourself.

Arizona's cultural experiences are as rich as its natural beauty. Winslow offers a glimpse into the region's history at the Old

Trails Museum, which showcases artifacts and exhibits related to the town's past and its connection to Route 66. For a deeper understanding of Native American culture, the Hopi Cultural Center, located about 90 miles from Winslow, provides insights into the traditions and history of the Hopi people. You can learn about Hopi pottery, weaving, and farming techniques that have been passed down for generations.

At the Grand Canyon, the Desert View Watchtower is a cultural and architectural highlight. Designed by Mary Colter, the watchtower offers stunning views of the canyon and features murals by Hopi artist Fred Kabotie, which depict Hopi legends and traditions. The Grand Canyon's visitor centers also offer educational exhibits about the geology, ecology, and history of the canyon, making it a great opportunity for learning as you explore.

When it comes to dining, Winslow offers a few unique spots that capture the spirit of Route 66. The Turquoise Room at La Posada Hotel is one of the most well-regarded restaurants in the area, serving up Southwestern cuisine with a modern twist. Their menu features local ingredients and offers a fine dining experience in a historic setting. For something more casual, Falcon Restaurant serves hearty American diner fare, perfect for a quick meal before hitting the road again.

At the Grand Canyon, dining options vary from casual cafes to fine dining. The El Tovar Dining Room at the historic El Tovar Hotel offers a refined menu with dishes like roasted duck and fresh fish, along with stunning views of the canyon. For a quick bite, the Bright Angel Restaurant serves up classic

American meals in a relaxed setting, while the Canyon Village Market is perfect for grabbing snacks and sandwiches if you're planning to hike or picnic.

A highlight of the Grand Canyon is, of course, watching the sunrise or sunset. Mather Point and Hopi Point are popular spots for catching the changing colors of the canyon as the sun rises or sets, but for a quieter experience, try Yaki Point or Lipan Point. Watching the first light hit the canyon walls is a magical experience that you'll never forget.

Historical highlights in the region include the Petrified Forest National Park, located about an hour and a half from Winslow. This park features colorful fossilized wood, ancient petroglyphs, and sweeping desert vistas. The Painted Desert, which runs through the park, is a stunning stretch of badlands known for its vibrant colors, making it a great stop for nature lovers and history buffs alike.

Guided tours are a great way to learn more about the region's history and natural beauty. In Winslow, guided tours of Meteor Crater are available, offering fascinating insights into the crater's formation and impact on the environment. At the Grand Canyon, guided ranger programs are offered throughout the year, covering topics like the park's geology, wildlife, and Native American history. Helicopter tours are also available for those who want to see the canyon from a different perspective.

Educational opportunities in the area include the Grand Canyon Field Institute, which offers a variety of classes and workshops on topics like geology, ecology, and Native American culture. These programs are perfect for travelers who want to deepen their understanding of the park while exploring its natural beauty.

Arizona's stretch of Route 66 offers a unique blend of history, culture, and natural wonders. Winslow's nostalgic charm and proximity to landmarks like Meteor Crater make it a must-visit destination, while the Grand Canyon's awe-inspiring beauty and educational opportunities ensure a memorable experience. From hiking and outdoor adventures to cultural immersion and fine dining, Arizona provides travelers with a well-rounded and enriching journey along Route 66.

California

California, known for its vibrant cities, stunning coastlines, and rich history, offers an unforgettable journey for travelers exploring the notable areas of Needles and Los Angeles. Both destinations, although distinct in their atmosphere, capture the essence of California's diverse landscapes and culture. Needles, located on the eastern edge of the state along Route 66, serves as a gateway to the Mojave Desert and is steeped in history. Los Angeles, on the other hand, is a sprawling metropolis famous for its film industry, beaches, and cultural landmarks. Together, these places offer a full California experience, combining desert adventure with urban exploration.

Getting to Needles is straightforward if you're driving along Route 66 or Interstate 40. If you're flying in, the nearest airport is in Las Vegas, about two hours away by car. Once in Needles, everything is accessible by car, and it serves as a great stopping point before heading deeper into California or exploring nearby natural wonders. For Los Angeles, travelers will most likely arrive at Los Angeles International Airport (LAX), a major hub with connections from around the world. From LAX, it's easy to rent a car or take public transportation to explore the city.

In Needles, one of the first places to visit is the Route 66 Mother Road Museum. This small, charming museum tells the story of the famous highway and its role in shaping American travel culture. You'll find vintage cars, historical photos, and memorabilia from Route 66's heyday. Just outside of Needles, the Mojave National Preserve offers incredible desert landscapes and outdoor activities. The Kelso Dunes are a must-see, and hiking to the top provides a panoramic view of the desert. The preserve is also home to Joshua trees, volcanic craters, and historic mining sites, making it a perfect destination for nature enthusiasts and history buffs.

Los Angeles, by contrast, is a bustling city with endless things to see and do. Start your exploration at Hollywood Boulevard, where you can see the Walk of Fame and visit the iconic TCL Chinese Theatre. The nearby Griffith Observatory offers stunning views of the city and the Hollywood Sign, as well as exhibits on astronomy. For art lovers, the Getty Center houses an impressive collection of European paintings and sculptures, as well as beautiful gardens and breathtaking views of the city.

Outdoor activities abound in both locations. In Needles, water sports are a popular way to enjoy the Colorado River, which runs along the town's edge. Rent a kayak or paddleboard and spend a day on the river, or simply relax by the water's edge and take in the scenic desert surroundings. Fishing is another popular activity here, with opportunities to catch bass and catfish. In Los Angeles, the outdoor activities are more varied, from hiking in the Santa Monica Mountains to surfing at the famous beaches of Malibu and Santa Monica. The Runyon Canyon Trail is a popular hiking spot for both locals and visitors, offering fantastic views of downtown LA and the Pacific Ocean.

Cultural experiences are a highlight of both Needles and Los Angeles, though in very different ways. Needles offers a slice of classic Route 66 culture, with roadside diners and motels that evoke the nostalgia of mid-20th century America. One such spot is the Wagon Wheel Restaurant, a local favorite where you can enjoy hearty diner fare. In Los Angeles, the cultural scene is as diverse as the city itself. Visit Olvera Street, a historic area that celebrates the city's Mexican heritage with markets, restaurants, and festivals. The Los Angeles County Museum of Art (LACMA) is another cultural hotspot, showcasing art from around the world and often hosting live music and film screenings.

Dining options in Needles tend to be more casual but full of charm. The Juicy's Famous River Café is a local institution known for its friendly service and homestyle cooking. Try their burgers or classic breakfast dishes before heading out for a day of adventure. In Los Angeles, the culinary scene is world-renowned, offering everything from food trucks to fine dining. Head to Grand Central Market for a taste of LA's multicultural food offerings, from tacos to ramen. For a more upscale experience, République in Mid-Wilshire serves French-inspired cuisine in a beautiful, historic building.

Highlights in Needles include a visit to the El Garces Hotel, a historic train station that once served as a stop for the Santa Fe Railway. The building is being restored and is a fascinating glimpse into the past. From Needles, you can also take a scenic drive along Route 66, stopping at places like Oatman, Arizona, where wild burros roam the streets, and Kingman, known for its Route 66 museums and retro charm.

In Los Angeles, a highlight is the Santa Monica Pier, where you can ride the Ferris wheel, play arcade games, or just stroll along the beach. For a unique tour of the city, consider taking a Hollywood Homes tour, where you can see the homes of the stars in Beverly Hills and the surrounding areas. If you're interested in history, visit The Autry Museum of the American West, which explores the history and culture of the American West through art, artifacts, and film.

Historical highlights in both areas are rich and varied. In Needles, the town's history is tied to both the railroad and Route 66. A stop at the Needles Regional Museum offers insight into the town's development and its connection to these historic routes. In Los Angeles, the Los Angeles Conservancy offers walking tours that delve into the city's architectural history, including Art Deco landmarks and historic theaters.

Guided tours are available in both Needles and Los Angeles, offering deeper insight into the history and culture of these areas. In Needles, guided tours of the Mojave National Preserve are a great way to learn about the desert's unique ecosystem and its history of mining and settlement. In Los Angeles, there are countless guided tours to choose from, including film studio tours at Warner Bros. or Universal Studios, where you can get a behind-the-scenes look at how movies and TV shows are made.

For educational opportunities, Los Angeles offers a wealth of museums and institutions. The California Science Center is a great place for families, with interactive exhibits on space exploration, biology, and more. The Natural History Museum of Los Angeles County also offers fascinating exhibits on the history of life on Earth, from dinosaurs to the present day.

A journey through Needles and Los Angeles captures the essence of California's varied landscapes and cultures. Whether you're exploring the quiet desert town of Needles along Route 66 or diving into the hustle and bustle of Los Angeles, you'll find endless opportunities for adventure, learning, and cultural immersion. From outdoor activities to world-class museums, these destinations offer something for every type of traveler.

CHAPTER 5

HISTORICAL LANDMARKS AND ATTRACTIONS

Iconic Motels and Diners

One of my favorite parts of any road trip is stopping at iconic motels and diners, where history, nostalgia, and comfort all seem to blend perfectly. These spots have become a must for travelers seeking a true taste of American roadside culture, especially along legendary highways like Route 66. The charm of staying at a classic motel or grabbing a bite in a retro diner is unmatched, and I've had some great experiences doing just that.

Let me take you on a little tour of some of the places I've discovered, and hopefully, you'll feel inspired to add these stops to your next journey.

The Blue Swallow Motel in Tucumcari, New Mexico, is the kind of place that immediately feels like a step back in time. You'll spot the glowing neon sign long before you reach the motel, a beacon of hospitality that's been lighting up Route 66 since 1939. The rooms are simple, cozy, and filled with vintage décor that keeps the spirit of the road alive. I remember checking in and being handed an actual room key with a tassel—a rarity these days. The best part is sitting outside your room in one of the metal chairs under the glowing lights, chatting with other travelers who, like you, are reliving a bit of American history. It's free to explore the grounds, but a night's stay will run you around $100. You can't miss it—located at 815 E Route 66 Blvd, Tucumcari, NM.

Another favorite stop of mine is The Big Texan Steak Ranch in Amarillo, Texas. If you're driving along I-40, you've probably seen the billboards advertising the "Free 72 oz. Steak"—but there's a catch. You've gotta eat the entire thing, plus the sides, in an hour to get it for free. I've never taken on the challenge, but it's fun to watch others try! The interior feels like a wild west saloon, and the portions are as big as Texas itself. Even if you're not in the mood for a food challenge, their menu has some fantastic barbecue and traditional American dishes. It's free to walk in, but if you're grabbing a bite, expect to pay around $20–$30 depending on your order. The restaurant is located at 7701 I-40 E, Amarillo, TX, right off the interstate, making it an easy stop.

When it comes to diners, there's something magical about sitting in a booth, sipping on a milkshake, and watching the world go by through the big windows. Lou Mitchell's in Chicago is one of those classic diners that's been around since 1923. Located at 565 W Jackson Blvd, Chicago, IL, it's right at the start of Route 66, making it the perfect place to fuel up before embarking on a road trip. When I was there, I couldn't resist ordering their famous fluffy pancakes, but they're also known for their omelets and homemade doughnut holes, which they hand out for free to all customers! It's a busy place, but the vibe is friendly and welcoming, making it a quintessential diner experience. Expect to spend about $10–$15 for a meal, and if you're lucky, you'll get to chat with some locals who can share their favorite Chicago haunts.

Another gem I discovered while cruising Route 66 is Delgadillo's Snow Cap Drive-In in Seligman, Arizona. This quirky little spot has been a staple since 1953, and stepping inside feels like walking into a time capsule. The place is covered in fun, bizarre memorabilia, and the staff loves to joke around with customers, making the whole experience lighthearted and fun. I had a classic burger and a shake, and I still remember the smile on my face as I sat in the old-fashioned car seats that have been turned into outdoor seating. The burgers are reasonably priced at about $6–$8, and the milkshakes are a must-try. It's free to wander around and take in all the decorations, but of course, you'll want to grab a bite while you're there. You'll find the diner at 301 AZ-66, Seligman, AZ, just off the highway.

Of course, not all the iconic motels are right along Route 66. The Wigwam Motel in Holbrook, Arizona, offers a unique lodging experience where you sleep in a giant teepee-shaped room. I stayed here during a road trip through the Southwest, and I can't recommend it enough. It's a piece of Americana that you won't find anywhere else. The rooms are simple but clean, with all the necessary amenities. Plus, they've got a collection of vintage cars out front that add to the charm. It's one of those places where you feel like the road trip itself is the destination. A night here costs around $80–$100, and it's located at 811 W Hopi Dr, Holbrook, AZ.

If you're looking for a real hidden gem, Midpoint Café in Adrian, Texas, is the perfect stop. As the name suggests, it marks the exact midpoint of Route 66, halfway between Chicago and Los Angeles. The café has a simple, no-frills charm, with a retro interior and friendly service. Their homemade pies are legendary, and I couldn't leave without trying a slice of their pecan pie, which lived up to the hype. It's a great place to stretch your legs, snap a photo by the Midpoint sign, and enjoy a piece of pie while reflecting on your journey. You'll find it at 305 W Historic Route 66, Adrian, TX, and it's an easy stop if you're already cruising the Mother Road.

For those traveling on a budget, many of these motels offer affordable rates compared to chain hotels, especially during off-peak seasons. Staying at a motel like the Blue Swallow or Wigwam not only saves you money but also gives you a richer experience of American road trip culture. And when it comes to diners, sticking to classic spots like Lou Mitchell's or Delgadillo's Snow Cap means you'll get hearty, inexpensive meals with a side of history and nostalgia.

These iconic motels and diners along Route 66 and beyond aren't just places to sleep or eat—they're destinations in themselves. From the neon glow of the Blue Swallow Motel to the quirky antics at Delgadillo's Snow Cap, these stops are a way to connect with the past and create lasting memories. Whether you're embarking on a cross-country road trip or just passing through, taking the time to visit these spots will make your journey all the more special.

Route 66 Signs and Murals

Traveling along Route 66 is like stepping into a living history book, and one of the most charming aspects of the journey is the abundance of vintage signs and murals that tell the story of the road's past. I've had the pleasure of taking this iconic route, and one of the most enjoyable parts of the trip is spotting these pieces of art that highlight not only the businesses they represent but also the heart of the communities they are a part of.

One of the most famous Route 66 signs is located in Seligman, Arizona. This small town is known as the "Birthplace of Historic Route 66" due to the efforts of Angel Delgadillo, who worked tirelessly to preserve the road after it was decommissioned. The Route 66 Roadside Attraction sign outside Delgadillo's Snow Cap Drive-In is a classic, and I couldn't resist snapping a picture. The bright red and yellow colors pop against the Arizona sky, and standing there, it's easy to imagine travelers from decades past taking the same photo. The sign itself is free to visit, and you can find it at 301 AZ-66, Seligman, Arizona. The whole town feels like a celebration of Route 66's heyday, so take your time walking around and soaking in the old-school charm.

Further along the route, in Amarillo, Texas, you'll come across one of the most famous and surreal public art installations along Route 66—Cadillac Ranch. While it's not exactly a traditional sign or mural, it's become a symbol of the route. There are ten Cadillacs half-buried nose-first into the dirt, and they're completely covered in layers upon layers of spray paint. The great thing about Cadillac Ranch is that it's interactive—you're encouraged to grab a can of spray paint and leave your own mark. I remember feeling a rush of excitement as I added a few colorful streaks to the cars, knowing that they'd soon be covered by the next set of visitors. It's free to visit and located just off I-40 at 13651 I-40 Frontage Road, Amarillo, Texas. There's no official entrance fee, and the installation is open 24/7, making it a must-see no matter when you're passing through.

Heading into Illinois, another place that stands out is Pontiac, a town known for its love of Route 66 murals. The Route 66 Hall of Fame & Museum at 110 W Howard St, Pontiac, IL, is surrounded by massive murals that depict the road's history, from its early beginnings to its pop culture status. I remember standing in awe, especially in front of the "Pontiac Loves Route 66" mural, which stretches across an entire building. It's a vivid, colorful tribute to the road, featuring classic cars and cheerful scenes of travelers. What I love about Pontiac is that the murals aren't confined to one area—you'll find them scattered around town, all free to enjoy. It's a great place to walk around, camera in hand, and get a real sense of how much this community embraces its Route 66 heritage.

In Tucumcari, New Mexico, the Blue Swallow Motel is a must-see for any fan of vintage signage. This neon-lit landmark is one of the most iconic along the route, and its bright blue swallows glowing in the night are an unforgettable sight. The sign itself has been meticulously maintained over the years, and seeing it flicker on as the sun sets is like watching history come alive. I stayed at the Blue Swallow during one of my trips, and seeing the sign up close was one of the highlights. Even if you're just passing through, make sure to stop and get a picture. The address is 815 E Route 66 Blvd, Tucumcari, NM. It's free to view the sign, though staying overnight will give you the full experience.

Of course, no trip down Route 66 is complete without seeing the famous "Get Your Kicks on Route 66" mural in Tucumcari. Located near the Tee Pee Curios shop at 924 E Route 66 Blvd, Tucumcari, NM, this mural captures the spirit of adventure that Route 66 inspires in travelers. The vintage cars, bright colors, and catchy slogan make it a perfect backdrop for photos. The shop itself is worth checking out, with its quirky selection of Route 66 memorabilia. There's no cost to see the mural, but it's hard to resist picking up a souvenir or two inside the shop.

Another spot that stands out is Galena, Kansas, home to the Route 66 Mural that showcases the history of the route through the state. This mural, located at 319 W 7th St, Galena, KS, is a tribute to the small town's role in the history of the Mother Road. The mural features bright colors and iconic imagery from the road's past. I remember walking around Galena and feeling like I had stepped back in time, with the quiet streets and the mural offering a glimpse into what the town might have looked like during Route 66's peak. It's free to view and makes for a great stop if you're looking to explore a quieter, less commercialized part of the route.

For those who appreciate quirky roadside attractions, the 66 Diner in Albuquerque, New Mexico, is a neon beacon of nostalgia. While the diner itself is a place to grab a bite (I highly recommend the milkshakes), its retro signage is an attraction in its own right. The bright neon lights and classic diner design make it feel like you've stepped into the 1950s. Located at 1405 Central Ave NE, Albuquerque, NM, this spot is easy to find and free to visit, though you'll want to sit down for a meal to truly soak in the atmosphere.

One of the things I've loved most about traveling Route 66 is the way that each mural and sign tells a story. Whether it's the neon glow of a motel or a hand-painted mural that celebrates a town's connection to the road, these pieces of art serve as mile markers on a journey that's as much about the past as it is about the present. Taking the time to stop and appreciate these signs and murals turns the trip into something more than just a drive—it becomes an experience rich with history and creativity.

If you're traveling on a budget, the great thing about Route 66's signs and murals is that they're almost all free to enjoy. You can spend the entire day photographing the art, walking around towns, and taking in the scenery without spending much more than the cost of gas and maybe a meal or two. It's one of the best ways to experience the road, allowing you to connect with its history without breaking the bank.

The signs and murals along Route 66 are much more than just roadside attractions. They're pieces of living history that make the journey itself as memorable as the destination. Whether it's the neon glow of the Blue Swallow Motel, the colorful murals in Pontiac, or the interactive art at Cadillac Ranch, each stop along the way tells a part of the Route 66 story, and I can't wait to see what new discoveries await on my next trip down the Mother Road.

Museums and Visitor Centers

As I traveled along Route 66, I discovered that some of the most enriching experiences came from visiting the numerous museums and visitor centers scattered along the way. These places not only serve as gateways to the history of this iconic highway but also provide fascinating insights into the communities that have thrived along its path.

One of my first stops was the Route 66 Museum located in Victorville, California. Tucked away on 16825 S D St, this museum is easily accessible from the I-15 freeway. Just take the D Street exit and follow the signs. The entrance fee is minimal—only $2 for adults—and it was worth every cent. Upon entering, I was immediately enveloped in the nostalgia of the road's glory days. The museum showcases a wide range of exhibits, including vintage cars, photographs, and memorabilia from the heyday of Route 66. Each display tells a story, and I found myself lingering over the old postcards that capture the charm of roadside attractions from decades past. There's also a gift shop where I couldn't resist picking up a few souvenirs. Spending a couple of hours here truly enriched my understanding of the road's history and its impact on American culture.

Next, I ventured to the Route 66 Visitor Center in Barstow, California. Located at 815 W Main St, it's conveniently positioned near the main route. The visitor center is free to enter and offers a wealth of information about the history of Route 66, including brochures and maps that highlight key attractions along the road. The staff was incredibly friendly and knowledgeable, eager to share tips about must-see spots. I appreciated the displays featuring vintage signage and artifacts, which provided a deeper appreciation for the cultural significance of the road. I spent some time chatting with the staff, who were more than happy to recommend other places to visit. It's a great place to gather your thoughts and plan the next leg of your journey.

As I continued my adventure, I made my way to the National Route 66 Museum in Elk City, Oklahoma. The address is 2717 E Hwy 66, and the museum is easy to find along the iconic highway. The entrance fee was a very reasonable $5, and I found that it provided access to a fantastic array of exhibits. The museum not only focuses on Route 66 but also includes sections dedicated to the history of transportation in America. I marveled at the vintage cars, road signs, and even a replica of a 1950s diner. One of the highlights for me was the section dedicated to the famous people who traveled the route, with stories and memorabilia that brought their journeys to life. I spent a couple of hours exploring the exhibits, taking photographs, and soaking in the ambiance. The staff members were passionate about the history of Route 66 and eager to answer any questions, making my visit even more enjoyable.

Moving on to Tulsa, Oklahoma, I couldn't miss the chance to visit the Oklahoma Route 66 Museum located at 222 N Main St. This museum offers a comprehensive look at the impact of Route 66 on Oklahoma's history and culture. The entrance fee was $7, and it was well worth it for the wealth of information contained within. The museum features interactive displays that allow visitors to engage with the history of the road, from its construction to its current status as a cultural icon. I particularly enjoyed the section dedicated to the music that has been inspired by Route 66. With its vibrant atmosphere and engaging exhibits, I spent hours exploring, learning about the road's significance, and even discovering some hidden gems in the gift shop.

A must-visit along the route is the Route 66 Hall of Fame & Museum in Pontiac, Illinois. Located at 110 W Howard St, this museum celebrates the history and culture of Route 66 through a variety of exhibits and artifacts. The entrance fee was $5, and I was immediately struck by the warmth of the space. The museum includes a great collection of memorabilia from the road's heyday, and I was fascinated by the stories of the towns that flourished because of the highway. One of my favorite parts was the gallery showcasing the artistic interpretations of Route 66 from local artists. It really highlighted how the road has inspired creativity in so many ways. I spent some time chatting with other visitors, sharing our favorite spots along the route, which added to the communal feel of the experience.

In Albuquerque, New Mexico, I found the Albuquerque Museum of Art and History, located at 2000 Mountain Rd NW. While not exclusively a Route 66 museum, it offers fantastic exhibitions that delve into the history of the city, including its connection to the iconic highway. The entrance fee is $4, and I was thrilled to find various exhibits highlighting the significance of Route 66 in Albuquerque's development. The museum hosts a variety of rotating exhibits, and I enjoyed viewing the local art that reflects the spirit of the road. I also loved wandering through the outdoor sculpture garden, where I found pieces that celebrate the rich history and culture of New Mexico. Spending an afternoon here was a perfect way to experience both art and history in a single visit.

In Winslow, Arizona, the Winslow Visitor Center at 523 W 2nd St is a great place to learn more about the town's unique Route 66 heritage. The visitor center is free to enter, and the staff was incredibly welcoming, eager to share the town's stories. Inside, I found information about local attractions and historical sites, including the famous "Standin' on a Corner" Park, which celebrates the Eagles song. I took a moment to enjoy the art installation at the park, capturing the essence of the town and its connection to the music industry. The staff also shared tips on local eateries, which I found invaluable. The visitor center is a lovely stop to gather insights and learn about the quirky character of Winslow.

As I reflect on my journey along Route 66, I realize that visiting museums and visitor centers added a depth to my experience that I hadn't anticipated. Each location offered a unique perspective on the history of the road and its significance to the towns it passes through. I found that taking the time to explore these cultural touchstones allowed me to connect with the journey in a way that made each stop more meaningful. From vintage cars to interactive exhibits and warm conversations with locals, these museums and centers provide a wonderful blend of education and enjoyment. So, if you find yourself on this legendary highway, I highly recommend taking the time to explore these enriching stops—they're truly the heartbeat of Route 66.

CHAPTER 6

CULTURAL EXPERIENCES ALONG THE ROUTE

Local Festivals and Events

Route 66 isn't just about scenic drives and nostalgic diners; it's also a vibrant cultural corridor where festivals and events bring local communities to life. These celebrations, scattered throughout the year, reflect the unique spirit of the regions they inhabit, giving travelers an authentic taste of American culture. Whether you're looking to experience traditional parades, food fairs, or music festivals, Route 66 has something for everyone. Here's a closer look at some standout festivals along the Mother Road.

The Route 66 Mother Road Festival, Springfield, Illinois (Late September)

As the days cool and the leaves begin to change, the Route 66 Mother Road Festival comes to life in Springfield, Illinois, every September. This festival celebrates the golden era of the road trip, drawing vintage car enthusiasts and history lovers from around the country. The fall season, with its crisp air and colorful landscape, adds an extra layer of charm to this event, making the atmosphere both nostalgic and festive.

The festival holds deep cultural significance, not just for car lovers but for those who cherish Route 66's role in American history. Springfield has long been a hub of this legendary road, and the Mother Road Festival is a nod to the highway's golden age when cars like the Ford Mustang or Chevrolet Impala were king. It's a time to celebrate the local heritage of road travel, Route 66 nostalgia, and all things automotive.

Visitors can expect to see over 1,000 vintage cars lining the streets, with plenty of live music, food trucks, and vendors selling everything from memorabilia to crafts. One of the highlights is the Friday night parade, where classic cars cruise through the city, revving their engines as onlookers cheer. Foodies will love the array of American comfort food, while music fans can enjoy performances that blend classic rock with country sounds.

If you're planning to attend, it's best to book accommodations in advance, as Springfield gets quite busy during this time. Comfortable shoes are a must, as you'll spend most of your day walking around admiring the cars. The festival is free to attend, though food and drink purchases can add up. Budget travelers can enjoy affordable meals from local vendors, and if you're a car enthusiast, early registration for the car show can offer a more immersive experience.

Crowds are a given at the Mother Road Festival, particularly during the parade and car show peak hours. To avoid the busiest times, arrive early in the morning or explore side streets during peak hours. Comparatively, while there are similar car shows across the U.S., this one stands out because of its deep connection to Route 66. Its location in Springfield gives it an authentic edge, making it a must-see for anyone driving the Mother Road.

Red Dirt BBQ & Music Festival, Tyler, Texas (Early May)

In early May, as spring blossoms across Texas, Tyler comes alive with the smell of smoked meats and the sounds of live country music during the Red Dirt BBQ & Music Festival. This festival marks the start of Texas' barbecue season and welcomes a wide variety of barbecue enthusiasts and music fans, making it a feast for the senses. The weather in May is typically warm but pleasant, perfect for outdoor gatherings.

Barbecue is a key part of Texas' cultural fabric, and this festival celebrates it in all its smoky, delicious glory. The festival not only highlights the state's best pitmasters but also brings together the community through its rich food traditions. Visitors will see the reverence Texans have for their craft, with vendors showcasing their skills over open fires and wood-smoked pits.

At the festival, you'll find endless rows of barbecue stands offering brisket, ribs, pulled pork, and more. Coupled with the food is an incredible lineup of Red Dirt musicians—a genre of country music deeply rooted in Texas and Oklahoma culture. Expect to see both rising stars and well-known names like Randy Rogers Band or Turnpike Troubadours gracing the stage, creating an atmosphere full of Southern charm and good vibes.

To make the most of the experience, bring sunblock and wear light clothing, as Texas in May can get quite warm by midday. Arrive early for the best seating near the main stage, and don't forget to grab your food tokens in advance to avoid long lines. While general admission tickets are affordable, food costs can add up if you plan on tasting several dishes. Budget travelers should look for early-bird ticket deals or stay in nearby budget accommodations to save on lodging.

Crowd-wise, the festival draws a big local crowd, especially later in the day when the main musical acts start. Try arriving earlier to sample the barbecue before the lines grow long, or stay late to enjoy the music as the sun sets over Texas.

Tulsa International Mayfest, Tulsa, Oklahoma (Mid-May)

Tulsa's downtown bursts into color every May during the Tulsa International Mayfest, a celebration of art, culture, and community. Mid-May sees warm days and comfortable evenings, perfect for enjoying this outdoor festival. As the flowers bloom and the city comes to life, the festival's artistic energy blends perfectly with the season.

Mayfest has been a staple of Tulsa's cultural calendar for over 40 years, making it one of the city's most anticipated events. It brings together artists, musicians, and performers from across the country, showcasing a rich variety of talent and creativity. This festival is deeply connected to Tulsa's arts scene and reflects the city's broader efforts to support and celebrate creative expression.

Visitors can explore hundreds of art booths featuring everything from handmade jewelry to fine paintings, enjoy live music on several stages, and indulge in a variety of street food.

For families, there are interactive art exhibits and activities for kids, making it an event everyone can enjoy. You might also catch performances from local theater groups or street performers, adding to the festival's lively atmosphere.

The best way to enjoy Mayfest is to bring cash for the food and art booths, wear comfortable walking shoes, and plan to spend most of your day outside. Many of the art exhibits and performances are free to attend, though if you're on a tight budget, make sure to bring snacks or eat before arriving to keep costs down. Parking in downtown Tulsa can be tricky during the festival, so consider using rideshare services or public transport to get there.

Tulsa Mayfest does draw significant crowds, particularly on the weekend, so if you're looking to avoid the hustle, consider visiting during a weekday. Compared to other art festivals, Mayfest is unique in its deep connection to local culture while still maintaining an international flavor, giving it an eclectic yet distinctly Tulsa vibe.

Route 66 Blowout, Sapulpa, Oklahoma (Early June)

In early June, as summer begins to heat up, the small town of Sapulpa, Oklahoma, hosts the Route 66 Blowout, an annual car show and street festival celebrating the town's connection to the historic highway. The early summer season means warm weather, blue skies, and plenty of outdoor activities, making this a perfect time for a road trip.

Sapulpa, located right on Route 66, takes pride in its deep ties to the Mother Road, and the Blowout is a tribute to that heritage. This event brings the community together to honor the cars, businesses, and culture that grew along Route 66. It's a celebration of small-town pride, filled with family-friendly fun.

At the Blowout, visitors will find classic car displays, a bustling street market with local vendors, and plenty of activities for kids. The festival often features live music, food trucks, and contests for the best cars, adding to the lively, festive atmosphere. One of the highlights is the parade of classic cars that runs through downtown Sapulpa, bringing Route 66 to life.

To get the most out of the Route 66 Blowout, arrive early to secure a good parking spot and beat the heat. Wear a hat and sunscreen, as you'll be outdoors most of the day. The event itself is free, but you'll want to bring money for food and drinks, as local vendors offer plenty of tempting treats. Budget travelers can enjoy most activities without spending much, making this an affordable yet enjoyable stop along Route 66.

Crowds tend to gather around the main street where the car show takes place, so if you're looking to avoid the busiest spots, explore the market and food areas during the midday lull. While there are plenty of Route 66 festivals, the Blowout stands out for its small-town charm and its strong sense of community, making it an essential stop for those traveling the Mother Road.

These festivals along Route 66 provide not only entertainment but also an intimate look into the heart of the communities that make up the fabric of the highway. Whether you're a fan of vintage cars, great music, delicious food, or local art, there's something for everyone along the way.

Music and Art Scene

The music and art scene is vibrant and lively, full of creativity and expression. In cities and towns, you'll find a mix of different styles and genres that reflect the local culture and history.

When it comes to music, you'll hear everything from rock and blues to country and folk. Many cities host live music events where local bands play at bars, parks, and festivals. These events are great for experiencing the talent in the community. If you're lucky, you might catch a performance in a small venue where the atmosphere is cozy and intimate. People gather to enjoy the music, dance, and sometimes even sing along.

In larger cities, you can find big concerts featuring well-known artists. These events often take place in arenas or outdoor stadiums, drawing crowds from all around. Attending a concert is not just about the music; it's about the energy of the crowd and the excitement in the air.

The art scene is just as rich. Galleries showcase the work of local artists, displaying everything from paintings and sculptures to photography and mixed media. Many artists draw inspiration from their surroundings, creating pieces that tell stories about their communities. Walking through an art gallery can be a wonderful experience. You might find unique pieces that make you think or feel something special.

Street art and murals are also important parts of the art scene. Many neighborhoods have colorful murals that brighten up the walls of buildings. These artworks often carry messages about social issues or celebrate local history. Walking through these neighborhoods is like taking a tour of creativity, where every corner offers something new to see.

Art festivals are popular events where artists gather to showcase their work. These festivals often feature live art demonstrations, workshops, and activities for all ages. It's a great way to meet artists, learn about their techniques, and even buy some beautiful pieces to take home.

If you want to dive deeper into the local culture, consider taking an art class or a music lesson. Many community centers offer affordable classes where you can learn to play an instrument, paint, or try your hand at photography. It's a fun way to express your creativity while meeting new people.

The music and art scene is a wonderful part of any community. It brings people together, fosters creativity, and creates an atmosphere full of life and color. Whether you enjoy attending concerts, visiting galleries, or simply exploring the streets, there is something for everyone to enjoy in this vibrant world of art and music.

Native American Heritage Sites

Exploring Native American heritage sites is a fascinating way to learn about the rich cultures and histories of Indigenous peoples. These sites can be found across the United States and offer unique experiences that connect you to the past.

One of the most notable places to visit is Monument Valley in Utah and Arizona. The landscape is breathtaking, with towering red rock formations that have been featured in many movies. You can take a guided tour led by Navajo guides who share stories about the land and their traditions. Walking through the valley, you can feel the spiritual connection the Navajo people have with this beautiful area.

Another significant site is the Taos Pueblo in New Mexico. This ancient village is made of adobe and has been continuously inhabited for over a thousand years. You can take a guided tour to learn about the history, customs, and lifestyle of the Taos people. The views from the pueblo are stunning, and the experience gives you a glimpse into their daily life and culture.

The Indian Pueblo Cultural Center in Albuquerque, New Mexico, is another great spot to learn about Native American heritage. The center has exhibits showcasing the history and art of the 19 Pueblo tribes. You can also enjoy traditional Native American food in their restaurant. The center often hosts events and performances, where you can see traditional dances and music, making it a lively place to visit.

In South Dakota, the Crazy Horse Memorial is a must-see. This massive sculpture honors the Lakota leader Crazy Horse and represents the pride of Native Americans. While the sculpture is still being completed, the visitor center has exhibits that tell the story of Native American history and culture. It's inspiring to see such a significant work in progress and to learn about the values and traditions of the Lakota people.

Another important site is the National Museum of the American Indian in Washington, D.C. This museum is dedicated to preserving and showcasing the history and culture of Native Americans. The exhibits include artifacts, art, and films that tell the stories of different tribes. The museum often hosts cultural events, workshops, and performances, making it an engaging place for visitors of all ages.

Visiting these heritage sites is not just about seeing beautiful landscapes or artifacts; it's about understanding the deep connections that Native American peoples have with their land and traditions. Each site offers a chance to learn about their stories, values, and ways of life.

When visiting these sites, it's important to be respectful and open-minded. Take the time to listen to the stories shared by guides and participate in any cultural activities offered. This will enrich your experience and help you gain a deeper appreciation for Native American heritage.

Exploring Native American heritage sites is a meaningful journey that connects you to the rich cultures and histories of Indigenous peoples. Whether you are admiring stunning landscapes, learning about ancient traditions, or participating in cultural events, each visit leaves you with a greater understanding and respect for these vibrant communities.

CHAPTER 7.

FOOD AND DRINK

Must-Visit Diners and Cafes

Route 66 is not just a highway; it's a journey through Americana, and the diners and cafes along the way are a reflection of this vibrant culture. From classic roadside diners to cozy cafes and high-end eateries, the culinary scene is as diverse as the landscape. Here's a comprehensive guide to must-visit diners and cafes on Route 66.

One of the most iconic spots along the route is the Lou Mitchell's in Chicago, Illinois. Known as the "Gateway to Route 66," this diner has been serving travelers since 1923. The atmosphere is bustling and welcoming, with vintage decor and a long counter filled with friendly staff. Breakfast is a highlight here, and you can expect to pay around $10-$15 for a hearty meal. Don't miss the signature pancakes, which are fluffy and served with a variety of toppings. The complimentary donut holes and coffee served as you wait for your meal are a delightful touch that makes every visit special.

As you make your way to Missouri, stop at The Roadhouse in St. Louis. This casual restaurant has a rustic vibe with wooden beams and a relaxed atmosphere. Prices here range from $12-$25 for main courses. The Roadhouse is famous for its BBQ, particularly the smoked brisket sandwich, which is tender and bursting with flavor. Pair it with a side of homemade coleslaw for the perfect meal.

In Kansas, you must visit Baxter Springs' Route 66 Cafe. This charming little diner is adorned with Route 66 memorabilia, giving it a nostalgic feel. The pricing is budget-friendly, with meals ranging from $7-$15. The breakfast burrito is a local favorite, packed with scrambled eggs, cheese, and salsa, all wrapped in a warm tortilla. The cozy atmosphere makes it an ideal stop for families or those looking for a casual dining experience.

In Oklahoma, Tally's Good Food Cafe in Tulsa is a must. The atmosphere is lively and family-friendly, with a retro diner feel. Expect to spend about $10-$20 per person. The cafe is well-known for its hearty breakfast options, but the chicken-fried steak served with gravy is a standout dish that you shouldn't miss. It's a true taste of Southern comfort food and perfectly showcases the local culinary traditions.

As you continue your journey to Texas, stop by Big Texan Steak Ranch in Amarillo. This establishment is famous not only for its massive 72-ounce steak challenge but also for its vibrant cowboy-themed decor. Prices vary widely, but you can enjoy a meal here for $20-$40. Their ribeye steak is exceptionally tender and cooked to perfection, making it a favorite among meat lovers. The lively atmosphere and friendly service add to the experience, making it a fun stop for all travelers.

Further along in New Mexico, The Blue Heron Restaurant in Santa Rosa offers a charming dining experience. The ambiance is warm and inviting, perfect for a romantic dinner or a cozy gathering. Prices range from $15-$30 for main courses. The blue corn enchiladas are a signature dish, featuring locally sourced ingredients and a rich, flavorful sauce that highlights the unique taste of New Mexican cuisine.

In Arizona, don't miss The Diner in Winslow. This classic diner has a retro vibe and is adorned with Route 66 memorabilia. Prices are very reasonable, typically around $10-$15 per meal. The signature dish is the "Standing on a Corner" burger, named after the famous song. It's a delicious, juicy burger topped with fresh ingredients that perfectly encapsulates the spirit of Route 66.

As you reach California, make a stop at The Apple Pan in Los Angeles. This diner has a nostalgic charm, with wooden booths and counter seating. Expect to spend about $15-$25 for a meal. The hickory burger is their signature dish and is grilled to perfection, served with a side of their famous fries. The diner's history and classic charm make it a fantastic final stop on your Route 66 journey.

Traveling along Route 66 offers a culinary adventure filled with diverse flavors and experiences. Each diner and cafe has its own unique story, and sampling the local cuisine is a highlight of any trip. Whether you're enjoying a classic breakfast at Lou Mitchell's or tackling the 72-ounce steak challenge at the Big Texan Steak Ranch, these dining spots will leave you with delicious memories of your journey along the Mother Road.

Regional Cuisine Highlights

Traveling along Route 66 isn't just a journey through beautiful landscapes and historic towns; it's also a tantalizing culinary adventure. Each region along the route showcases its own unique flavors and dishes, offering a rich tapestry of American cuisine. Here are five regional cuisine highlights that I discovered on my travels, each with its own story and signature dish that left a lasting impression.

In Illinois, my first taste of deep-dish pizza was an experience that changed my perspective on pizza entirely. I visited a renowned pizzeria in Chicago, where the wait for a table was filled with the irresistible aroma of baking crust and bubbling cheese. When my deep-dish pizza finally arrived, I marveled at its towering height. The crust was thick and flaky, encasing layers of mozzarella, fresh tomatoes, and savory sausage. Each bite was a hearty explosion of flavors, with the sauce sitting on top, keeping everything moist and delicious. This pizza is a meal in itself, and I could hardly finish my slice, but I relished every mouthful.

Moving into Missouri, I encountered the famous Kansas City barbecue. My first stop was a well-known barbecue joint in Kansas City that was bustling with energy. The signature dish here was the burnt ends, which are tender chunks of brisket that are smoked to perfection. The sweet and tangy sauce clung to each piece, creating a sticky, flavorful experience. As I bit into the smoky, juicy meat, I was transported to barbecue heaven. The tender texture and bold flavors left me craving more. It's a dish that truly embodies the spirit of Kansas City and its deep-rooted barbecue culture.

Continuing south into Oklahoma, I couldn't resist trying chicken-fried steak, a staple in Southern cuisine. I found a charming diner in Tulsa that served this beloved dish. When it arrived, it was a generous portion, golden brown and smothered in creamy gravy. The first bite was a revelation—the crispy exterior gave way to a tender piece of beef, and the gravy added a rich, comforting flavor. It felt like a warm hug on a plate. This dish is hearty and filling, perfect for anyone looking to indulge in classic Southern comfort food.

As I journeyed into Texas, I was eager to sample Tex-Mex cuisine. My first experience was at a bustling taqueria in Amarillo, where the vibrant colors and lively atmosphere set the tone. I decided to try the breakfast tacos, a local favorite. The soft tortillas were filled with scrambled eggs, spicy chorizo, and fresh salsa, creating a delightful combination of textures and flavors. Each bite was a party for the senses, and I understood why breakfast tacos are a beloved tradition in Texas. This dish perfectly encapsulates the fusion of Mexican and American flavors.

Finally, in New Mexico, I had my first taste of blue corn enchiladas at a cozy restaurant in Santa Fe. The dish was beautifully presented, with vibrant colors from the blue corn tortillas topped with a rich red chile sauce. As I took my first bite, the flavors danced on my palate. The unique taste of blue corn added a depth that I hadn't experienced before. Coupled with melted cheese and a hint of spice, it was a dish that I couldn't get enough of. This meal truly reflected the region's culinary heritage and was a memorable highlight of my trip.

While indulging in these regional delights, it's essential to consider health tips for those with allergies and dietary restrictions. If you have gluten sensitivities, be sure to ask about gluten-free options, as many diners are becoming more accommodating. For dairy allergies, don't hesitate to inquire about dairy-free alternatives, especially when it comes to sauces and dressings. If you are vegetarian or vegan, many restaurants offer plant-based dishes, particularly in larger cities along Route 66. Always communicate your needs to the staff, who are generally eager to help you find something delicious that fits your dietary restrictions.

Embarking on this culinary journey along Route 66 opened my eyes to the diverse flavors that represent American culture. Each dish tells a story, and the experiences I had while tasting them made my travels unforgettable. Whether you are a seasoned foodie or just looking to try something new, these regional cuisine highlights will surely enrich your journey on the Mother Road.

Best Places for Roadside Snacks

Traveling along Route 66 is not just about the big attractions; it's also about enjoying the little moments, especially when it comes to food. Roadside snacks are a fun and tasty way to break up your journey and discover local flavors. Here are some of the best places to stop for snacks that will make your trip even more enjoyable.

One of the best spots for a quick bite is in Illinois, where you can find the famous Maggie's Diner. This charming little diner is known for its fresh, homemade pies. When I visited, I couldn't resist trying a slice of their cherry pie. It was served warm, with a flaky crust and sweet, juicy cherries inside. Pair it with a scoop of vanilla ice cream, and you have the perfect treat to enjoy while sitting on their outdoor patio.

As I made my way into Missouri, I discovered a roadside stand selling pulled pork sandwiches. This spot is a local favorite, and the aroma of the smoked meat wafting through the air drew me in. I ordered a sandwich topped with coleslaw and tangy barbecue sauce. The tender pork was full of flavor, and the crunchy slaw added a nice texture. It was the kind of snack that kept me energized for the rest of my drive.

In Oklahoma, you can't miss the chance to stop at a route-side food truck known for its frito chili pie. This dish is simple yet delicious, made with Fritos corn chips, chili, and cheese. When I took my first bite, the salty chips combined with the spicy chili created a comforting, satisfying snack. Enjoying this dish in the warm sun while chatting with locals made for a great experience.

In Texas, there are many small convenience stores that serve homemade jerky. I stopped at one that had a variety of flavors, from classic beef to spicy turkey and even teriyaki. The jerky was tender and packed with flavor, perfect for snacking on during a long drive. I loved sampling the different kinds and ended up buying a bag to take with me on my journey.

While in New Mexico, I came across a roadside shop that sells biscochitos, which are traditional New Mexican cookies flavored with anise and cinnamon. I had never tasted anything like them before. They were slightly crunchy on the outside and soft inside, with a wonderful flavor that reminded me of the holidays. The friendly shop owner offered me a free sample, and I couldn't resist buying a box to enjoy later.

As you travel along Route 66, keep an eye out for these roadside snack spots. They offer a wonderful way to experience the local culture and flavors. Always be open to trying new things, as you never know what delicious treats you might discover along the way. Whether it's a sweet treat or a savory bite, roadside snacks can add a delightful touch to your road trip adventure.

CHAPTER 8.

ACTIVITIES AND ADVENTURES

Outdoor Activities and Scenic Stops

Traveling along Route 66 is not just about the iconic diners and roadside attractions; it also offers plenty of outdoor activities and scenic stops that let you experience the beauty of America. Here are some great outdoor activities to enjoy, along with their addresses and how to get there.

One fantastic outdoor activity is hiking at Petrified Forest National Park in Arizona. This park is famous for its colorful petrified wood and beautiful desert landscapes. The park is located at 1 Park Rd, Petrified Forest, AZ 86028. To get there, take Interstate 40 and exit at Route 180. Once inside the park, there are several trails, like the Blue Mesa Trail, that are easy to navigate and offer stunning views. Don't forget to bring plenty of water and your camera to capture the incredible scenery.

If you're looking for a fun family-friendly stop, consider visiting Sand Dunes Recreation Area in Colorado. This area has the tallest sand dunes in North America and is perfect for sandboarding and picnicking. The address is 11999 State Hwy 150, Mosca, CO 81146. To reach it, take Highway 160 to Highway 150. Once you arrive, you can rent sandboards or simply enjoy a walk through the dunes. It's a unique experience that the whole family will love.

In New Mexico, the Bandelier National Monument is a must-visit for those interested in Native American history and beautiful landscapes. The address is 15 Entrance Rd, Los Alamos, NM 87544. To get there, take US Highway 84/285 to NM-4. Once you arrive, you can explore ancient cliff dwellings and enjoy various hiking trails. The Main Loop Trail is popular and showcases stunning views of the canyon and the historic dwellings.

For a relaxing scenic stop, visit the Route 66 State Park in Missouri. The address is 97 Morton Rd, Eureka, MO 63025. This park offers picnic areas, walking trails, and beautiful views of the Meramec River. To get there, take Interstate 44 to exit 261. You can spend some time walking along the river or enjoying a picnic under the trees, soaking in the peaceful atmosphere.

Make sure to check out Devil's Lake State Park in Wisconsin for stunning natural beauty. The park is located at S5975 Park Rd, Baraboo, WI 53913. To reach it, take I-90/94 to Highway 12. This park offers hiking trails, swimming, and rock climbing. The East Bluff Trail is popular for its breathtaking views of the lake and surrounding cliffs. Bring a picnic to enjoy by the water after your hike.

These outdoor activities and scenic stops along Route 66 provide an excellent way to experience the natural beauty and cultural history of America. Whether you enjoy hiking, relaxing by the water, or exploring unique landscapes, there is something for everyone on this iconic road. Be sure to pack your gear and get ready for an adventure filled with stunning sights and memorable experiences.

Historic Roadside Attractions

Driving along Route 66, you'll discover a treasure trove of historic roadside attractions that tell the story of America's past. Here are some must-see attractions, along with their addresses and directions to help you find your way.

One of the most iconic stops is the Route 66 Museum located at 222 N 1st St, Victorville, CA 92392. This museum showcases the history and culture of Route 66, featuring exhibits of classic cars, photographs, and memorabilia. To get there, take Interstate 15 and exit at Bear Valley Road, then follow the signs to Victorville. It's a great place to learn about the significance of the Mother Road.

Next, make your way to the World's Largest Rocking Chair in Fanning, Missouri. This giant chair stands proudly at 13797 Highway 66, Fanning, MO 65466. To visit, take Interstate 44 and exit at Highway 66. The chair is hard to miss, and it makes for a perfect photo opportunity! While you're there, check out the nearby gift shop for unique souvenirs.

In Oklahoma, stop by the Blue Whale of Catoosa at 2600 U.S. Highway 66, Catoosa, OK 74015. This whimsical roadside attraction features a giant blue whale that you can walk on and take pictures with. To reach it, take Highway 66 from Tulsa, and you'll find the whale right off the road. It's a fun spot for families and a nostalgic piece of Americana.

Another fascinating spot is the Cadillac Ranch in Amarillo, Texas, located at 13651 I-40, Amarillo, TX 79124. This quirky art installation features a row of old Cadillacs buried nose-first in the ground. To get there, take Interstate 40 and look for the signs. Visitors are encouraged to bring spray paint to leave their mark on the cars, making it a fun and interactive experience.

Make sure to visit the Route 66 Archway in Lebanon, Missouri, found at 202 E Commercial St, Lebanon, MO 65536. This archway stands at the entrance of the historic Route 66 and is a symbol of the road's rich history. To find it, take Interstate 44 and exit at Highway 64. The archway is a great place to stop, take pictures, and learn about the significance of Route 66.

These historic roadside attractions along Route 66 offer a glimpse into America's past and create wonderful memories for travelers. Each stop has its unique charm and story, making your road trip not just a drive but an adventure through history. As you explore these attractions, take your time to appreciate the nostalgia and creativity that each one represents.

Adventure Sports Along the Route

Traveling along Route 66 offers more than just scenic views and historic sites; it's also a great place for adventure sports. Here are some exciting activities you can try, along with their addresses and directions to help you get there.

One popular adventure sport is white-water rafting on the Arkansas River in Colorado. The best spot to experience this is at Rafting Colorado, located at 305 Main St, Canon City, CO 81212. To get there, take U.S. Highway 50, and follow the signs to Canon City. This company offers various levels of rafting experiences, so whether you're a beginner or an expert, there's a perfect trip waiting for you.

If you enjoy hiking, you can head to Petrified Forest National Park in Arizona. The park is located at 1 Park Road, Petrified Forest, AZ 86028. To get there, take Interstate 40 and exit at Route 180. The park has several trails that lead you through beautiful landscapes and past stunning petrified wood. Don't forget to bring plenty of water and snacks for your hike.

For thrill-seekers looking for something unique, try zip-lining at Ozark Zipline Company in Branson, Missouri. The address is 17405 MO-13, Branson, MO 65615. To reach it, take Highway 65 and exit at Branson. You'll glide through the trees with amazing views of the Ozark Mountains. This is a fantastic way to feel the rush while enjoying nature.

If you want to try rock climbing, head to Garden of the Gods in Colorado Springs, Colorado. The address is 1805 N 30th St, Colorado Springs, CO 80904. To get there, take Interstate 25 and follow the signs to the park. The stunning red rock formations offer great climbing routes for all skill levels. You can either climb on your own or join a guided tour.

Another exciting option is biking along the Illinois River Trail in Illinois. The trail starts at 3000 N 53rd Ave, Peoria, IL 61604. To get there, take Interstate 74 and exit at Farmington Road. This scenic trail runs along the river and offers beautiful views. You can rent bikes nearby or bring your own for a fun day outdoors.

These adventure sports along Route 66 provide an opportunity to experience the thrill of the outdoors while enjoying the beauty of America's landscapes. Whether you prefer rafting, hiking, zip-lining, climbing, or biking, there's something for everyone along the route. So grab your gear, hit the road, and make unforgettable memories as you explore the adventurous side of Route 66.

CHAPTER 9.
THE LEGACY OF ROUTE 99

Pop Culture References

Route 66 is not just a famous highway; it is also a part of pop culture that has inspired songs, movies, and books over the years. Traveling along this iconic road, you will find many references to its history and charm in various forms of media.

One of the most famous references is the song "Get Your Kicks on Route 66." This classic song, written by Bobby Troup in 1946, celebrates the joy of traveling along this highway. Many artists, including Nat King Cole and the Rolling Stones, have covered it. Listening to this song while driving on Route 66 can make your journey feel more special and connected to the American experience.

You might also recognize Route 66 from the animated movie "Cars." In this film, the characters visit a fictional town called Radiator Springs, which is inspired by real towns along Route 66. The movie highlights the charm of small towns and the importance of community, which reflects the spirit of the highway. If you have children, it's a great idea to watch this movie before your trip to get everyone excited about the adventure.

Another popular reference is the TV show "Route 66," which aired in the 1960s. The show followed two young men traveling across the country in a Corvette, exploring America and meeting interesting people along the way. It captured the essence of freedom and adventure that Route 66 represents. Watching a few episodes can give you a sense of the fun and excitement of road trips.

You can also find Route 66 mentioned in books and novels. One notable book is "On the Road" by Jack Kerouac, which describes the author's travels across America, including parts of Route 66. The book is a key part of the Beat Generation and reflects the search for meaning and adventure in life. Reading this book can inspire you to embrace the spirit of exploration during your trip.

When visiting Route 66, keep an eye out for landmarks and attractions that are featured in pop culture. For example, the Route 66 Museum in Victorville, California, showcases the history and impact of the highway on American culture. Here, you can learn about how Route 66 has influenced music, film, and art over the decades.

As you drive along the route, you will see quirky signs and roadside attractions that add to the charm of your journey. Places like the giant Route 66 sign in Santa Monica or the Cadillac Ranch in Amarillo have become famous through social media and popular culture. Stopping at these spots can make your trip even more enjoyable and memorable.

Route 66 is rich with pop culture references that enhance the experience of traveling this historic highway. From songs and movies to books and museums, you can find many ways to connect with the culture and history of Route 66. Embrace the adventure, take lots of pictures, and enjoy the journey!

Route 66 in Film and Literature

Route 66 has made its mark not only on the map but also in film and literature, capturing the hearts of many through its iconic charm and stories. This historic highway symbolizes adventure, freedom, and the American spirit, making it a perfect backdrop for various creative works.

One of the most famous songs about Route 66 is "Get Your Kicks on Route 66," written by Bobby Troup in 1946. This catchy tune has been performed by many artists, including Nat King Cole and the Rolling Stones. The song invites listeners to explore the highway and enjoy the beautiful sights along the way. As you drive on Route 66, listening to this song can make your journey feel even more special.

In film, Route 66 has appeared in numerous movies. A beloved example is "Cars," a popular animated film produced by Pixar. In this movie, a racecar named Lightning McQueen finds himself in a small town inspired by real places along Route 66. The film highlights the importance of community and friendships, encouraging viewers to appreciate the little towns that dot the highway. Watching "Cars" can be a fun way to get excited about your own trip along Route 66, especially if you have kids.

Another significant film is "The Grapes of Wrath," based on John Steinbeck's classic novel. The story follows a family traveling from Oklahoma to California during the Great Depression. While the film does not focus exclusively on Route 66, it captures the spirit of those who traveled the highway in search of a better life. It showcases the struggles and hopes of

American families, giving you a glimpse into the historical context of the time.

Route 66 is also mentioned in the book "On the Road" by Jack Kerouac, which is a key work of the Beat Generation. The book tells the story of a group of friends traveling across the country, exploring America and searching for meaning in their lives. Although it does not exclusively follow Route 66, it embodies the spirit of adventure and spontaneity that the highway represents. Reading this book can inspire you to embrace your own journey along Route 66.

Additionally, many novels, poems, and essays reference Route 66 as a symbol of travel and exploration. These literary works often describe the diverse landscapes and unique experiences found along the highway. They highlight the charm of small towns, the beauty of the open road, and the stories of the people you meet along the way.

As you travel Route 66, keep an eye out for landmarks and attractions that are featured in these films and books. Visiting places like the Route 66 Museum in Victorville, California, can deepen your appreciation for the highway's cultural impact. Here, you can learn about its history and how it has influenced artists, writers, and filmmakers throughout the years.

Route 66 has been a significant inspiration in film and literature. From songs and animated films to classic novels, the highway has captured the imagination of many. As you embark on your own adventure, immerse yourself in these cultural references and let them enhance your experience on this legendary road. Enjoy the journey and the stories that await you along the way!

Ongoing Preservation Efforts

Ongoing preservation efforts for Route 66 are crucial to maintaining its charm and history. Many people and organizations are dedicated to keeping this iconic highway alive for future generations.

One of the main goals of these efforts is to restore old buildings and signs that reflect the unique character of Route 66. This includes diners, motels, and gas stations that have been around since the heyday of the road. By repairing and preserving these places, communities can keep their history alive and attract visitors who want to experience the authentic Route 66 vibe.

Several local groups, like the Route 66 Association, work hard to promote awareness about the importance of preserving this historic highway. They host events, such as festivals and car shows, where people can come together to celebrate Route 66. These events not only draw attention to the road but also raise funds for preservation projects.

Another important aspect of preservation is education. Many organizations develop educational programs that teach people about the history and significance of Route 66. Schools and local communities often participate in these programs, learning about the road's impact on American culture and the economy. By educating younger generations, preservationists hope to inspire them to value and protect this historic route.

In some areas, state and local governments are also taking action. They recognize the economic benefits of a preserved

Route 66. By investing in restoration projects and promoting tourism along the highway, communities can boost their local economies. This means more jobs and opportunities for residents.

Volunteers play a big role in these preservation efforts. Many people donate their time to help clean up and restore sites along the highway. They might paint a historic diner, plant flowers, or even organize cleanup days to remove litter from the roadside. These volunteer efforts create a sense of community and pride among residents.

There are also digital initiatives aimed at preserving Route 66. Some organizations create websites and social media pages that share stories, photos, and memories from the road. This helps keep the spirit of Route 66 alive, even for those who may not be able to visit in person.

When you travel along Route 66, you can contribute to these preservation efforts. Consider stopping at local businesses, eating at diners, and staying in historic motels. By supporting these establishments, you help ensure they can continue to operate and preserve their unique history.

Ongoing preservation efforts for Route 66 involve restoring historic sites, educating the public, and encouraging community involvement. These efforts are vital to keeping the spirit of the Mother Road alive. By participating in and supporting these initiatives, you can help protect the legacy of Route 66 for future travelers to enjoy.

CHAPTER 10.

PRACTICAL INFORMATION

Money matters and Currency Exchange

When planning a trip along the historic Route 66, understanding money matters is essential for making the most of your adventure. Let's explore the currency you'll be using, where to exchange it, tips on budgeting, local pricing trends, and some resources to help you navigate your finances effectively.

Currency Overview
While the currency used in Italy is the Euro (€), the Route 66 stretches across the United States, where you'll be using the US Dollar (USD). The US Dollar is significant as it is one of the most widely recognized currencies globally, making transactions straightforward for travelers. It's essential to familiarize yourself with the current exchange rate before your trip, as this will help you budget accordingly.

Currency Exchange Options
Exchanging currency is easy along Route 66. Here are some of the best options:

1. Banks: Major banks in the United States often provide currency exchange services. Look for national chains like Bank of America or Chase. They usually offer competitive rates, but check if they charge a service fee.

2. Exchange Offices: Currency exchange offices are found in larger cities and tourist areas, including places like Chicago and Los Angeles. While they might offer convenience, their rates can be less favorable, and fees may apply.

3. ATMs: Using ATMs is often the most cost-effective way to withdraw cash in USD. Look for ATMs that belong to your bank's network to avoid high fees. Always choose to be charged in USD instead of local currency to get the best rate.

Budgeting Tips
When it comes to budgeting for your Route 66 trip, it helps to break down expenses into categories. Here's an overview of average costs for different types of travelers:

1. Accommodation:
   - Budget: $50–$100 per night (hostels or motels)
   - Mid-range: $100–$200 per night (chain hotels or boutique inns)
   - Luxury: $200+ per night (high-end hotels or resorts)

2. Meals:
   - Budget: $10–$20 per meal (fast food, diners, or casual restaurants)
   - Mid-range: $20–$50 per meal (local favorites or nice cafes)
   - Luxury: $50+ per meal (fine dining experiences)

3. Transportation:
   - Renting a car costs around $30–$100 per day, depending on the model and rental agency.

- Gas prices fluctuate, averaging $3–$4 per gallon, so plan your fuel budget accordingly.

4. Activities:
  - Free attractions: Many roadside stops and national parks
  - Paid attractions: $10–$50 for entry fees to museums or guided tours

Local Pricing Insights
Pricing can vary along Route 66, especially between urban and rural areas. For instance, larger cities like Los Angeles might have higher accommodation and dining costs compared to smaller towns like Flagstaff or Winslow. Be mindful of seasonal pricing trends; summer months typically see a rise in hotel rates and attractions due to tourist influx. Additionally, always check for hidden costs, such as parking fees in cities or extra charges for activities.

Resources and Tools
To help manage your finances during your Route 66 trip, consider these useful resources:

1. Budgeting Apps: Apps like Mint or YNAB (You Need A Budget) can help track expenses in real time.

2. Currency Converters: Websites like XE.com provide up-to-date currency conversion rates, ensuring you know how much you're spending.

3. Local Guides: Websites like TripAdvisor and Yelp can help you find dining options that suit your budget and preferences.

By understanding currency exchange options, setting a realistic budget, and utilizing helpful resources, you can make the most of your journey along Route 66. This iconic route is rich in history and adventure, and being prepared will enhance your experience. Enjoy the ride and the memories you'll create along the way.

Language and Communication

When traveling along the iconic Route 66, communication is key to enhancing your experience. While English is the primary language spoken throughout the United States, the rich tapestry of cultures along this historic road brings a variety of languages and dialects to the forefront, with notable influences from Italian and German. Understanding these languages and their nuances can significantly enrich your journey and help you connect with locals.

Language Overview

The Route 66 corridor primarily features English, but as you travel through diverse cities and towns, you might encounter communities where Italian and German have a noticeable presence. For instance, areas with a rich immigrant history may have Italian and German-speaking populations, particularly in urban centers. In addition, you might hear regional dialects and slang that reflect the local culture, adding to the vibrant communication landscape of the route.

Basic Greetings and Polite Phrases

Familiarizing yourself with basic greetings and polite phrases in both Italian and German can go a long way in showing respect to the local culture. Here are some essential phrases, along with phonetic pronunciations to assist you:

In Italian:
- Hello: Ciao (chow)
- Please: Per favore (pair fah-vo-ray)
- Thank you: Grazie (graht-see-ay)
- Excuse me: Scusi (skoo-zee)

In German:
- Hello: Hallo (hah-loh)
- Please: Bitte (bi-teh)
- Thank you: Danke (dahn-keh)
- Excuse me: Entschuldigung (ent-shool-dee-goong)

Useful Phrases for Travelers
As you navigate your Route 66 adventure, these practical phrases can be invaluable. Here are some categorized phrases that will help you in various situations:

Ordering Food:
- I would like...: Vorrei... (Italian - vor-ray) / Ich hätte gerne... (German - ikh hett-eh gair-neh)
- What do you recommend?: Cosa ci consiglia? (Italian - koh-sah chee kon-see-lyah) / Was empfehlen Sie? (German - vahs em-fay-len zee)

Asking for Directions:
- Where is...? : Dov'è...? (Italian - doh-vay) / Wo ist...? (German - voh ist)

- Can you help me?: Può aiutarmi? (Italian - pwah ah-you-tar-mee) / Können Sie mir helfen? (German - kuh-nen zee meer hel-fen)

Making Purchases:
- How much is this?: Quanto costa questo? (Italian - kwan-toh koh-stah kwes-toh) / Wie viel kostet das? (German - vee feel koh-stet dahs)
- I would like to buy this.: Vorrei comprare questo. (Italian - vor-ray kom-prah-ray kwes-toh) / Ich möchte das kaufen. (German - ikh merk-teh dahs kow-fen)

Seeking Assistance:
- I need help.: Ho bisogno di aiuto. (Italian - oh bee-zoh-nyoh dee ah-you-toh) / Ich brauche Hilfe. (German - ikh brow-khe hil-feh)

Language Learning Resources
To help you quickly pick up essential phrases before and during your trip, consider utilizing some effective language learning resources. Phrasebooks such as "Italian Phrasebook" and "German Phrasebook" by Lonely Planet offer handy references. Mobile apps like Duolingo and Babbel provide interactive learning experiences tailored to travelers. Websites like Memrise and Pimsleur also offer tailored content to help you master key phrases for your Route 66 journey.

Cultural Insights
Language and communication extend beyond words; they also encompass cultural nuances. In both Italian and German cultures, using formal and informal language can signal respect and understanding. For instance, addressing someone

with "Sie" in German denotes respect, while "du" is more casual. Additionally, pay attention to body language and eye contact, as they vary across cultures. In many cases, maintaining eye contact signifies engagement and respect.

Multilingual Assistance

While English is the dominant language across Route 66, many tourist attractions, hotels, and restaurants have staff who speak multiple languages. English-speaking staff can be found at major landmarks and in bustling urban centers. To find these services, look for signs indicating multilingual support or simply ask at the front desk of your hotel. It's a good practice to inquire politely if you need assistance in a specific language.

Respect and Appreciation

As you journey along Route 66, embracing the local languages and cultures shows respect and appreciation for the communities you visit. Learning and using basic phrases not only facilitates communication but also opens doors to meaningful connections. Locals often appreciate the effort, which can lead to richer interactions and a deeper understanding of the culture.

By equipping yourself with essential phrases, understanding cultural nuances, and respecting the local languages, your Route 66 adventure will be not only enjoyable but also enriched by the connections you make along the way. Whether you're ordering a meal at a diner or asking for directions, these efforts will enhance your travel experience and create lasting memories.

Safety and Health

As you embark on your journey along Route 66, understanding the language and communication landscape can enhance your travel experience. While English is predominantly spoken throughout the United States, you might encounter Italian and German influences, especially in areas with rich immigrant histories. These languages add a unique layer to the cultural fabric of the places you'll visit, reflecting the diversity of communities along this historic road.

Language Overview
Route 66 stretches across various states, primarily where English is the main language. However, areas with significant Italian and German heritage can offer glimpses of these languages, especially in regions like Chicago, which has a strong Italian community, or places like St. Louis, where German heritage is prominent. You may hear regional accents and dialects that showcase the local culture, making your journey all the more fascinating.

Basic Greetings and Polite Phrases
Learning a few essential phrases can help you connect with locals and show respect for their culture. Here are some basic greetings and polite phrases in Italian and German, along with phonetic pronunciations to guide you:

In Italian:
- Hello: Ciao (chow)
- Please: Per favore (pair fah-vo-ray)
- Thank you: Grazie (graht-see-ay)

- Excuse me: Scusi (skoo-zee)

In German:
- Hello: Hallo (hah-loh)
- Please: Bitte (bi-teh)
- Thank you: Danke (dahn-keh)
- Excuse me: Entschuldigung (ent-shool-dee-goong)

Useful Phrases for Travelers
As you navigate the various experiences along Route 66, having a list of practical phrases can be incredibly helpful. Here are some categorized phrases for different situations:

Ordering Food:
- I would like...: Vorrei... (Italian - vor-ray) / Ich hätte gerne... (German - ikh hett-eh gair-neh)
- What do you recommend?: Cosa ci consiglia? (Italian - koh-sah chee kon-see-lyah) / Was empfehlen Sie? (German - vahs em-fay-len zee)

Asking for Directions:
- Where is...? : Dov'è...? (Italian - doh-vay) / Wo ist...? (German - voh ist)
- Can you help me?: Può aiutarmi? (Italian - pwah ah-you-tar-mee) / Können Sie mir helfen? (German - kuh-nen zee meer hel-fen)

Making Purchases:
- How much is this?: Quanto costa questo? (Italian - kwan-toh koh-stah kwes-toh) / Wie viel kostet das? (German - vee feel koh-stet dahs)

- I would like to buy this.: Vorrei comprare questo. (Italian - vor-ray kom-prah-ray kwes-toh) / Ich möchte das kaufen. (German - ikh merk-teh dahs kow-fen)

Seeking Assistance:
- I need help.: Ho bisogno di aiuto. (Italian - oh bee-zoh-nyoh dee ah-you-toh) / Ich brauche Hilfe. (German - ikh brow-khe hil-feh)

Language Learning Resources
To help you master these essential phrases before your trip, consider using some effective language learning resources. Phrasebooks such as "Italian Phrasebook" and "German Phrasebook" from Lonely Planet can be handy references. Mobile apps like Duolingo and Babbel offer interactive lessons that cater to travelers. Websites like Memrise and Pimsleur also provide tailored content to help you learn phrases specific to the Route 66 area.

Cultural Insights
Understanding cultural nuances in language and communication is vital when interacting with locals. In Italian and German cultures, formality can play a significant role. For example, in German, addressing someone with "Sie" denotes respect, while "du" is used among friends. Also, body language and eye contact can vary. In many cases, maintaining eye contact is seen as a sign of engagement and respect, while in some cultures, prolonged eye contact might be considered impolite.

Multilingual Assistance

Throughout Route 66, you'll find that many tourist attractions, hotels, and restaurants offer staff who speak multiple languages, including English. This multilingual support is particularly common in larger cities and tourist hotspots. To utilize these services effectively, look for signs indicating language assistance or simply ask at the front desk of your hotel if they have English-speaking staff available.

Respect and Appreciation
As you travel along Route 66, taking the time to learn a few key phrases can demonstrate your respect and appreciation for the local culture. Using these basic phrases not only helps in daily interactions but also opens doors to deeper connections with the community. Locals often appreciate when travelers make an effort to communicate in their language, fostering goodwill and enriching your experience.

By equipping yourself with essential phrases and understanding the cultural context of communication, your journey along Route 66 can be more meaningful. Embrace the opportunity to connect with locals, and you'll create unforgettable memories along this historic route.

Emergency Contacts

Traveling along Route 66 can be an exciting adventure, but it's also important to be prepared for emergencies. Understanding the emergency services available, knowing whom to contact, and having a plan can make all the difference if something unexpected happens.

Overview of Emergency Services
Emergency services along Route 66 encompass police, fire, and medical assistance. In urban areas, services tend to be more accessible, with police departments, fire stations, and hospitals readily available. In rural areas, response times might be longer, and services can be more limited. However, emergency responders in these regions are often well-trained and equipped to handle various situations. It's good to familiarize yourself with local resources as you travel through different towns and landscapes along the route.

Emergency Phone Numbers
Knowing key emergency numbers is essential. In the United States, the general emergency number is 911. This number can be dialed for police, fire, or medical emergencies throughout Route 66. In addition to this, here are specific numbers you should keep handy:

- Local police: Dial 911 or contact local precincts directly, which you can find online or through your travel guide.
- Ambulance services: Usually included under the 911 service, but you can inquire locally for specific services.
- Fire department: Contact local fire departments through the general emergency number.

- Mountain rescue services: For areas like the Rocky Mountains, local search and rescue teams can be reached via 911 or through park services.

Local Hospitals and Clinics
It's wise to know where local hospitals and clinics are located, especially in key towns along Route 66. For instance, in towns like Chicago, you have access to major hospitals such as Northwestern Memorial Hospital at 251 E Huron St, Chicago, IL 60611, which can be reached at (312) 926-2000. Further along the route, in Santa Fe, New Mexico, you might visit Christus St. Vincent Regional Medical Center at 455 St. Michael's Dr, Santa Fe, NM 87505, reachable at (505) 913-5000. Each of these facilities offers a variety of services, from emergency care to specialized medical treatment. Checking local resources for smaller clinics or urgent care facilities in other towns is also a good idea.

What to Do in an Emergency
In the event of an emergency, remain calm and take a few important steps. Start by calling 911 for immediate assistance. Clearly communicate your location, the nature of the emergency, and any other pertinent details, such as whether you or others are in danger. If there are language barriers, using simple English phrases can help, or you might consider using a translation app to facilitate communication. Make sure to have essential information readily available, such as medical history or allergies, especially if emergency responders need to make quick decisions about your care.

Travel Insurance and Assistance

Having travel insurance is vital for covering medical emergencies, evacuation, or trip interruptions. When choosing a policy, look for one that provides comprehensive coverage, including medical expenses and repatriation. Many insurance companies offer assistance hotlines that you can call for support during emergencies. Familiarize yourself with your policy details and carry a copy with you while traveling to ensure you can access help if needed.

Personal Safety Tips
When engaging in outdoor activities like hiking or skiing along Route 66, preparation is key. Always carry a first aid kit and let someone know your plans, including your expected return time. If you are venturing into more remote areas, consider traveling with a partner or group. It's essential to stay aware of your surroundings, carry plenty of water, and dress appropriately for the weather.

Cultural Considerations
Cultural norms can influence how emergencies are handled. In the United States, people are generally willing to help, but approaching someone for assistance politely and with a smile can go a long way. If you need help, be clear and respectful in your requests. Most locals will appreciate your effort to communicate and may go out of their way to assist you.

Personal Anecdotes
Imagine a traveler named Sarah, who was driving along Route 66 when her car broke down in a remote area. At first, she felt anxious, unsure of what to do. However, she remembered to remain calm and assessed her surroundings. She walked to a

nearby diner and politely asked for assistance. The locals were friendly and helped her contact a tow service. From this experience, Sarah learned the importance of staying composed and reaching out for help when needed. It reinforced her belief in the kindness of strangers along the route.

Resources and Tools
To help you stay informed and prepared, consider downloading emergency apps like "Emergency: Emergency Alerts" or "First Aid by American Red Cross," which can guide you through various situations. Additionally, local tourism websites often provide information on emergency contacts and services in the area. Carrying a physical map can also be useful if your phone loses signal in remote locations.

Being aware of emergency contacts and how to navigate potential issues along Route 66 ensures that you can focus on enjoying your adventure. With the right preparation, you can have a safe and memorable experience on this iconic road.

Useful Websites and Apps

Embarking on a journey along Route 66 is an adventure filled with iconic landmarks, breathtaking scenery, and vibrant culture. To make the most of your trip, utilizing the right apps can streamline your planning and enhance your experience, making your travels smoother and more enjoyable.

Overview of Essential Apps
When it comes to planning and navigating Route 66, a variety of essential apps can be invaluable. Transportation apps like Google Maps are great for navigation, while rideshare options like Uber and Lyft can help you get around without the hassle of parking. Accommodation apps such as Booking.com and Airbnb allow you to find unique places to stay, from cozy motels to charming guesthouses. For outdoor enthusiasts, apps like AllTrails and Gaia GPS can enhance your adventure by providing detailed trail information.

Hiking and Outdoor Apps
For those looking to explore the great outdoors, hiking apps are a must. AllTrails is a popular choice, offering extensive trail maps and user-generated reviews that help you choose the perfect hike based on difficulty, length, and scenery. Gaia GPS provides topographic maps and navigational tools, making it easy to stay on course even in remote areas. ViewRanger also offers trail mapping and augmented reality features that can enhance your experience by providing context about the landscape around you. These apps allow you to plan hikes, check trail conditions, and get weather forecasts, ensuring a safe and enjoyable outdoor experience.

Accommodation and Dining Apps

Finding the right place to stay and eat is crucial when traveling along Route 66. Apps like Booking.com allow you to compare prices and find accommodations that fit your budget, whether you're looking for a luxury hotel or a quaint roadside motel. Airbnb offers a unique selection of local stays that can give you a more immersive experience. When it comes to dining, TripAdvisor is an excellent resource for discovering local restaurants, reading reviews, and finding hidden gems along the route. With these apps, you can easily make reservations and ensure you don't miss out on the best local cuisine.

Language and Translation Apps

As you travel, especially if you venture into areas with diverse cultural influences, language and translation apps can be incredibly useful. Google Translate can help you translate signs, menus, and conversations, making it easier to communicate with locals. Duolingo offers fun and interactive language lessons that can help you pick up essential phrases before your trip. iTranslate is another handy app for quick translations, allowing you to navigate language barriers effortlessly.

Emergency and Safety Apps

Safety should always be a priority while traveling. Apps like First Aid by American Red Cross provide essential information on how to handle medical emergencies, including step-by-step guides on common first aid procedures. GeoSure Travel Safety offers insights into the safety levels of different areas, helping you make informed decisions about where to go. It's also smart to have travel insurance apps on hand to ensure you can access support if needed.

Cultural and Historical Apps

To enrich your journey, consider downloading cultural and historical apps that offer insights into Route 66's rich heritage. Apps like Dolomiti UNESCO provide information about cultural sites and landmarks along the route. You can also find walking tour apps that guide you through significant historical areas, sharing fascinating stories and facts about the places you visit. These resources can help you connect more deeply with the history and culture of the region.

Offline Capabilities

Given that some areas along Route 66 may have limited internet access, it's important to choose apps with offline capabilities. Download maps, guides, and other essential information before you embark on your journey to ensure you have access to critical resources even without a data connection. Many navigation and hiking apps allow you to save maps offline, so you can confidently explore without worrying about getting lost.

Tips for Downloading and Using Apps

To make the most of your travel apps, ensure your devices are fully charged before you start your day. Consider carrying a portable power bank for backup power, especially if you plan to use your phone for navigation and photography. Be mindful of data usage, particularly if you are traveling internationally, to avoid roaming charges. Download apps while connected to

Wi-Fi and check for updates to ensure you have the latest features and information.

By utilizing these apps, your journey along Route 66 can be transformed into a seamless and enjoyable experience. From planning your itinerary and navigating stunning landscapes to discovering local cuisine and rich culture, the right technology can enhance every aspect of your adventure. Happy travels!

CONCLUSION

As you prepare to embark on your journey along the iconic Route 66, it's important to reflect on the unique tapestry of experiences that await you. This legendary highway is more than just a road; it's a pathway through time, showcasing the stunning natural beauty, rich culture, and delicious culinary delights that define this beloved American route. From the expansive deserts of New Mexico to the lush forests of California, every mile offers a chance to explore breathtaking landscapes and connect with the diverse history of the towns you'll encounter.

Route 66 invites travelers to embrace the spirit of adventure, allowing you to immerse yourself in the stories of the people who have called this road home. I fondly remember my own journey along the route, where I stumbled upon a small diner in a forgotten town. The warmth of the locals, the aroma of freshly made pie, and the stories shared over coffee created a connection that transcended the typical travel experience. It's these moments of genuine interaction that can inspire a sense of wonder and appreciation for the natural world around us.

I encourage you to step outside your comfort zone and embrace the unknown. Whether it's hiking a challenging trail that leads to panoramic views or sampling local delicacies that ignite your taste buds, these experiences will enrich your journey. The rewards of trying something new often lead to personal growth and unforgettable memories that stay with you long after your trip ends.

While the iconic stops along Route 66, like the Grand Canyon or Santa Monica Pier, are undeniably captivating, I urge you to explore the hidden gems that lie off the beaten path. Venture into local markets, engage with artisans, and participate in community events to discover the authentic essence of the region. Often, these lesser-known spots yield the most memorable moments and give you a deeper understanding of the vibrant culture that thrives along this historic route.

As you navigate through this beautiful region, remember the importance of sustainable travel practices. Respecting the environment, supporting local businesses, and engaging in responsible tourism are essential to preserving the magic of Route 66 for future generations. Every effort you make contributes to the legacy of this remarkable journey.

To enhance your experience, consider planning ahead but also leave room for spontaneity. Some of the best adventures happen when you least expect them, so be open to detours and recommendations from locals. Engaging with residents not only provides insider knowledge about the area but also fosters connections that can lead to lifelong friendships.

I invite you to share your own stories and experiences from your travels along Route 66. Whether through social media or travel blogs, your insights can inspire fellow travelers and contribute to the rich narrative of this historic highway. The beauty of travel lies in its ability to create a community of explorers who share in the joy of discovery.

As you prepare for this adventure, let the allure of the open road beckon you. The memories you create along Route 66 will become part of your own story, a testament to the beauty of adventure and exploration. Embrace the journey, savor the moments, and cherish the connections you make. This is not just a trip; it's an opportunity to create lasting impressions that will resonate in your heart for years to come. Safe travels and happy exploring as you discover the wonders of Route 66!

MAP

Scan QR Code with device to view map for easy navigation

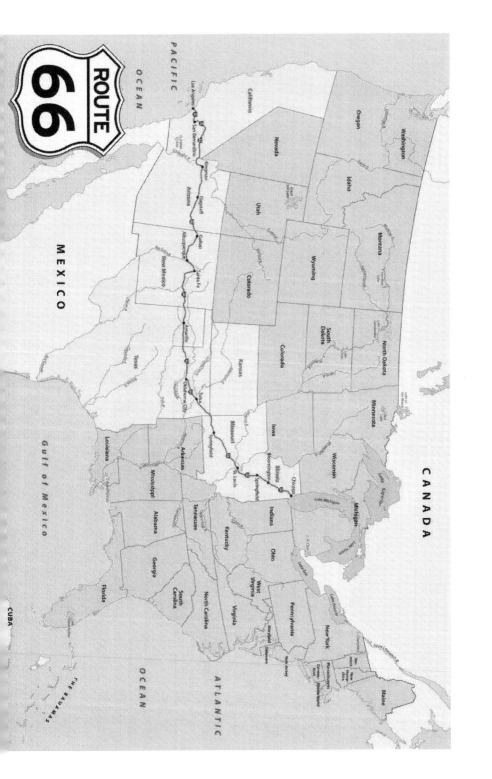

Bonus

NOTES

NOTES

NOTES

NOTES

Date:

NOTES

Made in United States
Troutdale, OR
12/27/2024

27287777R00097